# HOW SOCIAL SCIENCE CAN HELP US MAKE BETTER CHOICES

Optimal Rationality in Action

# HOW SOCIAL SCIENCE CAN HELP US MAKE BETTER CHOICES

## Optimal Rationality in Action

BY

**CHRIS BROWN**
*School of Education and Childhood Studies,
University of Portsmouth, UK*

United Kingdom – North America – Japan
India – Malaysia – China

Emerald Publishing Limited
Howard House, Wagon Lane, Bingley BD16 1WA, UK

First edition 2018

**Reprints and permission service**
Contact: permissions@emeraldinsight.com

**British Library Cataloguing in Publication Data**
A catalogue record for this book is available from the British
Library

ISBN: 978-1-78754-356-0 (Print)
ISBN: 978-1-78754-353-9 (Online)
ISBN: 978-1-78754-355-3 (Epub)

Printed and bound by CPI Group (UK) Ltd, Croydon, CR0 4YY

ISOQAR certified
Management System,
awarded to Emerald
for adherence to
Environmental
standard
ISO 14001:2004.

Certificate Number 1985
ISO 14001

INVESTOR IN PEOPLE

*Dedicated to the memory of Helen Brown and her 103 wonderful years and to Vincenza Holland a true stalwart in my life.*

# CONTENTS

# ABOUT THE AUTHOR

**Dr. Chris Brown** is Professor of Education at the School of Education and Childhood Studies, University of Portsmouth. Chris has a long-standing interest on how evidence can and should but often doesn't aid education policy and practice. To that end he has authored four books (including *Achieving Evidence-Informed Policy and Practice in Education: Evidenced* (2017) for Emerald), several papers and has presented and keynoted on the subject at a number of international conferences in Europe, Asia and North and South America. Chris's other principal research interest is centered on the use of semiotic theory and analysis to find better ways to understand the complex problems we often face. This is his second book focusing on this area (following on from *Scenes, Semiotics and the New Real: Exploring the Value of Originality and Difference* (2015) for Palgrave Macmillan).

In 2015, Chris was awarded the American Educational Research Association 'Emerging Scholar' award (Education Change SIG). The award is presented to an individual who, within the first eight years of their career as an educational scholar, has demonstrated a strong record of original and significant scholarship related to educational change. Chris was also awarded the 2016 AERA Excellence in Research to Practice award and the 2016 UCEA Jeffrey V. Bennett Outstanding International Research award.

# ACKNOWLEDGEMENTS

Realising this book would not have been possible without the commitment and support of Kim Chadwick, Emerald publisher extraordinaire. Thank you for your faith in me. Thanks also to Ruth Luzmore for engaging with me to discuss and flesh out many of the ideas. Finally, thanks, as ever, to my family for their continued patience as I demand 'just five more minutes to get this sentence finished' after saying exactly the same thing half an hour before.

# INTRODUCTION

In a world beset with problems, how can we encourage people to act differently? It seems almost daily that new studies emerge telling us how human action is causing planetary degradation, how changes to our diets and how more exercise could lead us to live longer healthier lives, or that financially we are in danger of returning to the debt-related crises of the previous decade. At the same time how many of us adjust our behaviour in response to such information? *How Social Science Can Help Us Make Better Choices* seeks to provide a new way to think about why people make the choices they do and, vitally, the role social science can play in response.

I use the book to explore people's reactions to optimal rational positions (or ORPs for short). ORPs are propositions that set out requirements for change. For example, the need to reduce carbon emissions to minimise the impacts of climate change is an ORP, as is the need for us to eat five items of fruit and veg a day. Other examples of ORPs include the suggestion that we should limit our alcohol consumption to 14 units per week[1] and that we should exercise for 30 minutes at least three times a week. Underpinning the book are two key arguments in relation to ORPs. The first is that, because they comprise a pragmatic coalescence of hard facts with a general desire to improve people's lives, ORPs present us with a substantive requirement to do something different. Second, we should want to pursue ORPs because they espouse the types of behaviours that will enable us to live healthier, happier or more productive lives; that can improve the lives and outcomes of others; or that can help us ensure social and environmental sustainability.[2]

At the same time what is or is not an ORP needs to be rigorously defined. I suggest we can think of ORPs typically emerging as a result of: (1) a robust and credible evidence base in relation to current or potential new behaviours; (2) a well-reasoned argument (or theory of change), which provides this evidence with meaning; (3) a social, moral or value-based imperative setting out the need for change based on this meaning (or conversely, the consequences of not changing) and (4) buy-in to this imperative from a range of credible stakeholders. These four steps can be illustrated using the example of human-led climate change. For instance, according to the Consensus Project[3] 97% of published papers with a position on global warming agree that global warming is happening (step 1). The authors of these papers also agree that climate change is caused by human action: specifically, the burning of fossil fuels, which adds additional greenhouse gases to the atmosphere, serving to trap more of the sun's heat and so warm the air, land and water (step 2). Global warming is shifting weather patterns and causing droughts and extreme weather events. It will also lead to a rise in the level of the oceans. Climate change has the potential to cause enormous damage to the global economy, the environment and our way of life for centuries to come. To minimise its impacts we should keep the global average temperature increase to well below 2°C above pre-industrial levels and ideally limit it to 1.5°C (Evans, 2017) (step 3); the 2015 Paris accord represents a global acknowledgement of the issue and a commitment by governments to reduce carbon emissions so as to limit warming to these levels (step 4).[4] These four steps together clearly provide a compelling argument for us to engage positively with the need to reduce carbon emissions. Similar analyses can also be provided for each of the ORPs mentioned above.

Because they represent a combination of facts and values, ORPs are often Kantian in nature – they involve 'should' type statements relating to a desired outcome: for instance, we *should* reduce carbon emissions, we *should* eat 'five a day', we *should* recycle more, we *should* drink less alcohol and so on. At the same time this 'should' will only hold for a given period – this is because each and every ORP is capable of shifting over time as new evidence emerges, new arguments are formulated to explain the evidence or new imperatives arise. ORPs are thus contextual and situational rather than universal: eventually counter positions are likely to be established (Vico, 2002). However, for any given point of time the current set of ORPs are likely to represent the best route we have for improving people's lives and achieving the type of society we want to live in.

At the same time, as we have seen in what is being described as the 'post truth' era, there is a danger that potential counter positions are conceived using untrustworthy evidence, and nourished with spin and scant disregard of the facts by those with vested interests. One example of this is the denial by some of the need to tackle human-led climate change (Evans, 2017); a view held by 6% of the public (Leiserowitz et al., 2017). As such, for any given accepted ORP it should be the role of scientists and researchers to work towards understanding how it can be implemented and maintained, to challenge false positions and where appropriate to only support genuinely new ORPs to emerge and take hold.

At its core, therefore, this work is grounded in the humanist tradition. Like Petrarch[5] I believe that our ethical approach should be shaped by an understanding of what can help us live a virtuous life: i.e. of knowledge of what can help us stay healthy, and that promotes sustainable actions. Correspondingly there is a role for social scientists and researchers to go beyond simply producing knowledge and towards actively seeking to achieve positive action in a world facing a multitude of problems. In Petrarch's time (1304–1374) Europe suffered from the Black Death, was entering the 100 years' war, while at the same time the church was grappling with the issue of *Avignonese papacy*. In modern times we face a wealth of issues, ranging from obesity to environmental degradation, around which there is a general consensus that urgent change is needed. Nonetheless, the approach presented here hopes to provide a smarter and more effective way to achieve action than through words alone. Whereas Petrarch sought to rely on 'eloquence' to achieve 'virtue' by 'moving the will of the hearer',[6] the approach set out in this book recognises that, in a world of echo chambers, it is increasingly difficult to get alternative arguments heard by those with entrenched views. As such I seek to show how ORPs can be attained by understanding what is needed to change people's perspectives and behaviours; and once this understanding has been reached a plan of action can then be put in place to help achieve this change. These two requirements, I argue, are totally within the reach and the purview of social scientists.

To describe the approach in the appropriate level of detail, the book is divided into six chapters. In Chapter 1, I outline the notion of optimal rationality, a model of rationality that seeks to explain why people can choose sub-optimal outcomes and yet still make rational choices. Representing a refashioning of Kantian and Aristotelian rationality, optional rationality can be used to identify the existence of rationality 'gaps' in relation to ORPs: in other words used to identify why people may not behave in accordance with ORPs despite recognising the long-term benefits doing so would provide. While identifying rationality gaps is a good first step, in Chapter 2 I turn to the concept of semiotics to examine how such gaps can be filled. Semiotics is concerned with what things or concepts signify (intimate) to us. Semiotic approaches can also be used to explore the relationships we have with things or concepts. Correspondingly I argue that by understanding the meaning ORPs convey to people, the benefits they feel ORPs will provide and the difficulty people perceive they will face in acting in accordance with them, we can begin to understand whether ORPs are attractive enough for people to engage with rather than pursue other options. From this understanding we can then develop interventions designed to alter the perceptions people have in relation to ORPs.

In Chapters 3 and 4, I present the optimal rationality/ semiotic (ORS) approach in action, using a case study from education. In particular I show how through employing the ORS model I was able to understand why teachers from three schools in Hampshire (United Kingdom) were not engaging with the notion of evidence-informed practice as a means to improve teaching and student outcomes. Using this analysis, I subsequently worked with the executive principal of these schools to develop a year-long intervention designed to foster evidence-informed school improvement. At the end of the intervention a second analysis was undertaken. Presented in Chapter 4, this second analysis illustrates that interventions can successfully be used to alter the significance of ORPs and as a result reduce rationality gaps. Building on from this work in Chapter 5, I argue that, while we typically have three ways of moving people to optimal rational behaviour (we can attend to the costs people associate with a specific ORP; we can do more to highlight the benefits of the ORP; or we can attend to the meaning associated with the ORP and so attempt to improve the attractiveness of any given ORP's brand), typically 'attractiveness' tends to be neglected. In response I use the chapter to look at how the semiotic phenomenon of 'scenes' can be employed to change the desirability of a given ORP and so people's wish to be associated with it. Finally, in Chapter 6 I explore the lessons from this work for social science and the potential ways in which researchers can develop approaches to maximise the types of ORP-related behaviour that can improve all of our lives.

A final point. This book is steeped in the notion of consumption. This is because I believe that behaviour change — especially in relation to ORPs — is fundamentally linked to how people currently consume and how they might consume moving forward. In other words behaviour change is about getting people to rethink and reallocate resource in a way that moves from one pattern of consumption to another: whether this be changing the amount of time spent on specific activities such as going to the gym or the money spent on specific goods. We all have only finite resource (time, money, energy) at our disposal — how we allocate this to specific activities matters if we are to solve the world's problems. Furthermore, in keeping with this focus on consumerism, I also frequently use within the book the potentially contentious term 'personal brand'. But using this term isn't an attempt to equate people with consumer objects or corporations. For me the notion of a personal brand is something that encapsulates the qualities and attributes that we believe make us who we are; they also simultaneously represent the things we would like others to recognise in us.

For example, one way to consider the idea of personal brand is to ask ourselves 'what qualities or attributes would my friends use to describe me'. We could repeat the question for our bosses or work colleagues, our family, our gym buddies, our neighbours and so on. If asking this for real the responses received, one would hope, would likely cover the qualities we believe matter and so attempt to enact and portray according to the relationship in question. In other words one would hope that people recognise and correctly interpret the meaning behind our deliberate actions. At the same time while not equating people with consumer objects we are all consumers and can generally recognise and take away from consumer brands the messaging they seek to convey to us. As such I argue that consumer brands can often also be used by people as a shorthand way to indicate specific qualities that form part of their personal brands. For example, where we purchase our groceries can indicate the extent to which food matters to us. Similarly our notion of personal style will be inherent in the clothes we buy. I return to this subject in Chapter 2 where I argue that the brand of an ORP and its relationship to our own personal brand will in part determine our engagement with it. In other words, determine whether we decide to consume in ways congruent with it.

## NOTES

1. See: https://patient.info/health/recommended-safe-limits-of-alcohol

2. Likewise ORPs can apply to governments and how they might foster and encourage behaviours and beliefs across society.

3. See: http://theconsensusproject.com

4. See: https://www.c2es.org/docUploads/cop-21-paris-summary-02-2016-final.pdf

5. See Petrarch (2008).

6. Also the work of other humanists such as Alberti who held similar perspectives in relation to art.

# CHAPTER 1

# AN INTRODUCTION TO OPTIMAL RATIONALITY

Although optimal rational positions (ORPs) represent real requirements for change, people do not always modify their behaviour to match what ORPs suggest *should* be done. Given that the pursuit of ORPs is likely to lead to long-term positive outcomes, does this mean that people are behaving irrationally? Or do we need to rethink our understanding of what counts as rational behaviour and, as a result, help people act more regularly in more beneficial ways? Assuming that the second of these possibilities is most likely I use this chapter to explore the concept of optimal rationality (OR). OR provides a framework for considering the choices people make. Vitally, however, OR also provides an alternative to popular conceptions of rationality that have so far failed to provide a basis for tackling those issues identified by ORPs.

One commonly used model of rationality that OR can be compared against is rational choice theory (RCT) (e.g. Green, 2002; Sen, 1990). A form of economics-based rationality, RCT has an underlying premise of methodological individualism. According to this premise, people's behaviour is characterised by their seeking to maximise the benefits (utility) and minimise the costs of pursuing a given goal (Green, 2002). As a consequence, individuals deliberate about the results of their actions according to how desirable these results are exclusively for themselves (Rose & Colman, 2007). While popular, RCT is subject to substantive critique. In particular, from studies that suggest individuals do not behave in ways that regularly and consistently maximise their benefits.[1] For instance, people often make do with 'good enough' solutions as opposed to optimal ones; they use short cuts and rules of thumb rather than seek out all the information required to achieve maximal utility; and people can rely on intuition or perception rather than analyse the data relating to their decisions (Bilalić, McLeod, & Gobet, 2008; Kahneman, 2003). Vitally however, people also typically exhibit bounded will power: individuals may engage in ways that are totally inconsistent with what will objectively serve them best in the long term (Jolls, Sunstein, & Aler, 1998). Similarly, people act with bounded self-interest: that is, they act and care about others, so sacrifice or limit the maximisation of their own interests (Jolls et al., 1998). An extension of the idea of bounded self-interest is that people can also actively 'team reason' and seek to maximise collective rather than the individual utility (Rose & Colman, 2007).

OR in contrast to RCT is grounded in philosophic rather than economic notions of rationality, in particular it is informed by the work of both Immanuel Kant (1724–1804) and Aristotle (384 BC–322 BC).[2] As a result, OR has a number of very specific characteristics: first and foremost OR is based on an acceptance of the Kantian idea that effective action can be determined if we apply reasoned argument to evidence: this is the very basis, in fact, of an ORP. At the same time OR rejects Kant's suggestion for how to ensure people act in ways believed to be effective: his notion of the

*universal moral imperative*. A moral imperative is something
that tells us uncategorically how to behave and is typically
signalled by the presence of an 'ought' (Scruton, 1982).
Moral imperatives are thus something we are intuitively
drawn towards, knowing that they are right – that we should
(i.e. 'ought') to do them. While accepting the idea that moral
imperatives can emerge from reasoned evidence-informed
arguments – as noted in the introduction, ORPs contain a
*should*-type statement – OR rejects any *universal* nature of
what seems right. This rejection has, first of all, a spatial/tem-
poral basis since any position that seems universally correct
now is simply right for a given place at a given point in time
(Latour, 1987). Second, a universal moral imperative, as its
name suggests, is an imperative that we all agree on. While
there are certainly beliefs that hold across individuals and
societies, given the strongly held positions of certain groups
it seems likely that for any ORP there will be some who do
not agree with it (Latour, 1987; Nozick, 1974; Williams,
1981). Some might disagree because the requirements of an
ORP represent a clash of values. Others, however, may
believe that the changes represented by the ORP will be dis-
advantageous to them: indeed, history is littered with groups
with vested interests – for instance tobacco firms and car
manufacturers – who have funded research studies with findings that suit viewpoints counter to ORPs (Evans, 2017).

OR is also informed by a repositioning of Aristotelian reasoning, which suggests that rationality may be exercised in
two ways: theoretically and practically. In other words, the
argument that rationality can occur both in terms of how we
think and what we do, with these forms of rationality existing separately and both being equally valid. While accepting
this division between what we think (or know) and what we
do, OR departs from key aspects of Aristotle's position in
three key ways. First, OR is grounded in the idea that in

modern Western societies we more or less have the freedom to choose how we act and behave. However, whereas Aristotle simply considers the activities at which people might direct their efforts in order to achieve happiness, OR considers the 'what we do' form of rationality in terms of both time and with regard to who might be affected by our actions. This is because OR argues that we can conceptualise and judge rational acts in terms of both *when* the result of actions are likely to materialise and *who* they will benefit or impact. The impact of rational acts thus ranges on the one hand from the individual (i.e. acts mainly benefit oneself rather than anyone else) to the universal (i.e. acts can lead to impact that benefits society as a whole) and on the other from short-term behaviour to that which also has benefits in the long term.

Second, while Aristotle considers virtue, OR argues that, whether in terms of when or who, in all cases rational behaviour is that which is concerned with achieving 'wellbeing'. This does not mean, however, the type of utility maximisation postulated by models of rationality such as RCT; instead OR suggests that acts to enhance well-being represent what individuals 'know' are 'needed' at a given point in time. Thus, while sometimes our day-to-day actions represent short-term responses to immediate needs, because they are designed to achieve a required state of well-being, they can nevertheless be regarded as more rational than acts that achieve greater well-being in the longer term, if this short-term well-being is considered by an individual to be more necessary. It is also clear, however, that only focusing on the short term can have detrimental longer term consequences. For example, an individual may decide to get drunk each evening to satisfy a short-term need, without considering or ignoring what impacts this might have for their longer term well-being, i.e. the serious health and social problems that arise from continuous drinking. These issues also ultimately have wider societal impacts, leading, for instance, to further pressure being placed putting on health services.

That our actions have wider consequences both for the long-term self and for others leads to the third departure from Aristotle. Although people have agency – we are free to choose what we want to do (e.g. Sartre, 2013), what we think about our potential and actual actions is framed by societal and cultural norms and beliefs: there are ways of thinking and behaving that are more and less preferred and viewed as more or less acceptable (Nozick, 2001; Petrarca, 2008; Saint Augustine, 2002). It is against these that we judge our behaviour and against which our behaviour is judged. This provides a situation in which we can do what we choose but we also know more generally what is considered to be the 'right thing'. Correspondingly OR incorporates within it society's role in imparting and instilling into individual's evidence, arguments and imperatives in order to provide a wider *milieu* within which their actions play out and are contextualised. This societal role may be thought of as providing normalising markers of what are considered to be appropriate – or *good* – behaviours which in turn establish a theoretical yardstick of reason against which people can judge their actions. It is clear then that ORPs, such as those detailed in the Introduction, can provide us through 'rationality of thought' a form of Kantian moral imperative: their purpose is to steer our thinking and so therefore our actions towards particular preferred paths that tend to objectively *maximise* welfare (i.e. welfare for everybody including ourselves, most typically in a period covering the longer term). Of course, not everybody will understand an ORP as representing the right thing, and ORPs can be rejected by some individuals and groups. Furthermore, because we are free to choose our actions we may not always act in conjunction with an ORP even though we know that doing so is the right thing to do, most often because an alternative may be more immediately appealing. When effective, however, OR positions serve to provide those checks that make sure we regularly engage in behaviour such as recycling and turning water taps and lights off, that we use hotel towels more than once, that we don't fly too often or offset our emissions when we do, that we exercise more or, in the example above, that we drink in moderation.

In summary, this refashioning of Aristotelian and Kantian rationality leaves us with the situation depicted in Figure 1.1: rational behaviour can be separated into thought and deed, individual and universal, long and short term and can involve achieving welfare across these. ORPs relate to maximising well-being in relation to a specific combination of these aspects of rationality; specifically, ORPs relate to well-being for the long-term self and/or the long-term universal. Individuals, while knowing about ORPs may not necessarily or regularly act in accordance with them if they perceive other needs to be greater or that, at a given point in time (e.g. in the short-term), other actions are likely to deliver them higher levels of welfare. Alternatively, if they do not subscribe to it, individuals or groups may reject an ORP and pursue an alternative path. An OR outcome on the other hand occurs when individual pursues their desires they do so in ways congruent with approaches suggested by ORPs, which ultimately involve maximising overall welfare. For example, revisiting the example above, drinking one drink each night will prove a better way to balance long- and short-term welfare than drinking four or five. Similarly eating more fruit and vegetables and less cakes and sugar will also keep us healthier in the long run, while balancing the joy we may gain from consuming the latter. In other words, in such situations we moderate our behaviour so

**Figure 1.1. An Overview of Potential Rational Behaviour.**

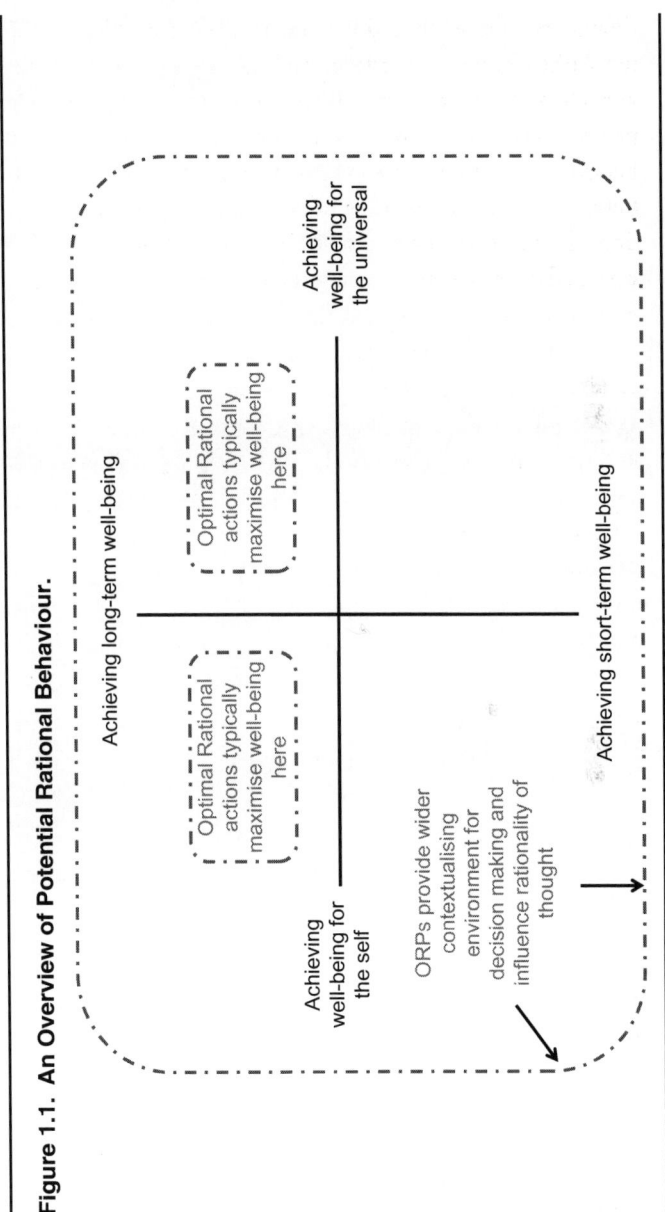

that if we (for example) eat cake one day, then for the next few days we don't in order to even out our actions and achieve a short- and long-term welfare balance. By recognising that abstaining can be a positive way to maximise welfare, engaging in it to bring ourselves into line with an ORP thus becomes a rational act, even if we have a short-term need to eat cake or drink more beer. In such cases our welfare is derived from recognising the dis-benefits of serving that need versus the benefits to us longer term.

In other cases such as recycling, the notion of the welfare of the individual becomes much more integrated with that of the collective.[3] Our short-term welfare reward for such action is often the understanding or recognition that we are doing something good (what Andreoni, 1990, describes as the 'warm glow'). Although we might not tangibly feel the short-term benefit (and indeed the walk to the recycling centre might be a bit of a drag), this is offset by recognising that we are contributing to a more sustainable environmental future for everybody – both now and moving forward. In this sense, the nature of OR is harmonious with the highest levels of Aristotelian happiness. This is because it may well take some individuals a great deal of mental and or physical effort to actively moderate their behaviour to move beyond acting in more short-term and individualistic way to feeling satisfied with a 'warm glow' reward that comes from acting regularly to drive longer term and collective welfare (Aristotle's notion of *training* virtuous behaviour). At the same time this work differs from thinkers such as Plato, Aristotle, Petrarca and Kant in that it accepts as reasonable that we often wish to pursue short-term pleasures. Nonetheless despite recognising the rationality of short-term self-interest, my aim is to help people pursue more optimal solutions when and where possible, since these are more beneficial long term, both personally and for society.

Understanding that sometimes individuals may know about ORPs but not engage in actions that cohere with them or may be rejecters of ORPs also help us to begin to consider the notion of 'rationality gaps'. Returning again to the example of human-led climate change, according to a 2017 report by Leiserowitz and colleagues, almost 6 out of 10 Americans are worried about climate change. The level of climate change denial meanwhile stands at 6%. These figures are at the same level as they were in 2012, which suggests that the US public is relatively well informed about the risk and reality of climate change as well as the need to reduce its likely impact: in other words, the ORP I established in the introduction tends to be acknowledged by the public. Yet while 4 out of 10 Americans think the odds that climate change will cause humans to become extinct are 50% or higher, and 7 out of 10 think it will harm future generations of people and plant and animal species, personal action is lacking (possibly exemplifying the tension I outline above between recognising an issue but not perceiving any tangible short-term benefits to addressing it). Of particular note is that of those surveyed by Leiserowitz, Maibach, Roser-Renouf, Rosenthal, and Cutler (2017) only 3% reported that their family and friends make 'a great deal of effort' and only 8% 'a lot of effort' to reduce global warming. A third (31%), however, did indicate that they engaged in 'a moderate amount of effort' to reduce global warming, but nearly half (48%) reported making 'no' or 'little effort'.

In terms of the ORP relating to human-led climate change, Leiserowitz et al.'s (2017) report shows that we can consider people's responses to ORPs according to their attitudes towards the ORP and their engagement with the

ORP. In other words, (1) whether individuals believe that the ORP is something that reflects how they and others should be behaving and (2) whether they are indeed acting in accordance with the ORP. Assuming that both beliefs/attitudes and actions can be assigned to the dichotomous categories of 'yes' or 'no', then this specific division of attitudes and actions can be represented by the $2 \times 2$ matrix set out in Figure 1.2.

As a result we can begin to consider individuals as belonging to one of four types as relates to any given ORP. Here 'Type 1' individuals are those who believe that the ORP represents the right thing to do and act in accordance with it. In other words, Type 1 individuals are achieving the OR situation of maximising welfare (i.e. welfare for the long-term self or long-term universal). 'Type 2' individuals are those who believe that the ORP represents the right thing to do but are yet to act in accordance with it: for instance, they may lack required knowledge, skills or resource to fully engage with the ORP. Type 2 individuals may also require a greater incentive to move away from engaging in more preferential activities such as long haul flights or heavy drinking. 'Type 3' individuals do engage in actions that cohere with the ORP but do not necessarily buy-in to the ORP. This may mean, for example, that the fact that their actions cohere with the ORP is simply coincidence or that their actions are driven by other factors (such as budget restraints). Alternatively it may mean that while they previously thought the ORP was a good thing they no longer believe this to be the case. Either way it seems likely that without positive buy-in to the ORP, the coherence of the actions of 'Type 3' individuals with the ORP is only likely to be temporary. Finally 'Type 4' individuals totally reject the ORP.

Allocating people to the types set out in Figure 1.2 also enables us to determine whether rationality gaps exist: in

**Figure 1.2.  Rationality Types.**

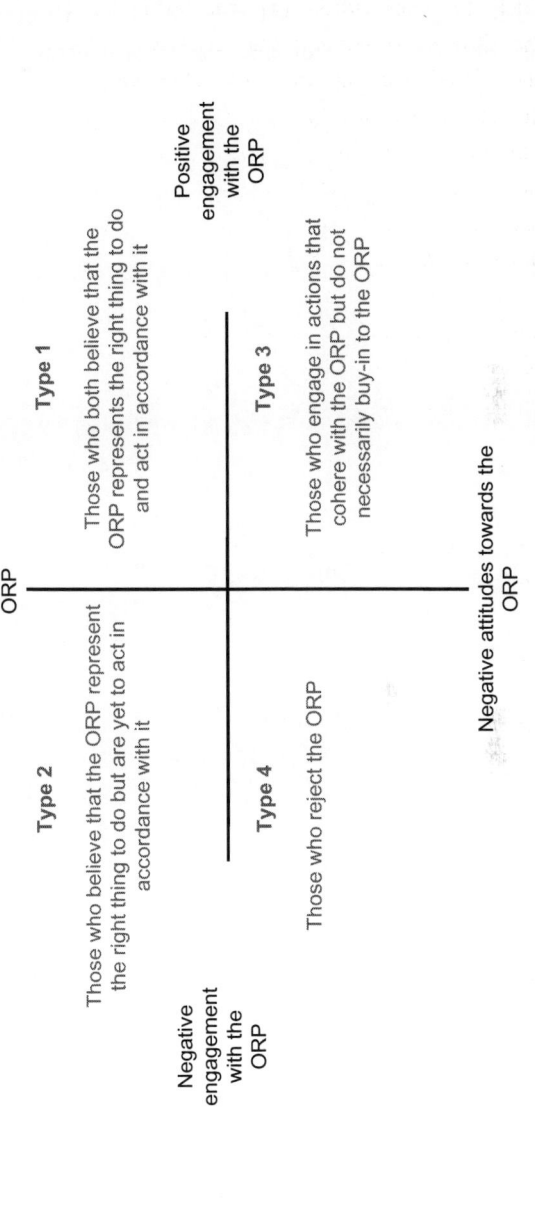

Positive attitudes towards the ORP

Positive engagement with the ORP

**Type 1**

Those who both believe that the ORP represents the right thing to do and act in accordance with it

**Type 3**

Those who engage in actions that cohere with the ORP but do not necessarily buy-in to the ORP

**Type 2**

Those who believe that the ORP represent the right thing to do but are yet to act in accordance with it

Negative engagement with the ORP

**Type 4**

Those who reject the ORP

Negative attitudes towards the ORP

other words whether outcomes could be more objectively beneficial than they currently are. This is because it is only 'Type 1' individuals who maximise well-being. While Types 2–4 are engaging in rational acts this will not be in accordance with what a given ORP suggests is required over the long term. For instance, considering Figure 1.1 people may instead be acting in the interests of the short-term self. And in the case of 'Type 3' individuals, their actions are likely to be temporary, and possibly, if disillusioned with the ORP, 'Type 3s' may also be supportive of other counter positions. Rationality gaps in essence then represent the proportional differences between those people who might be considered 'Type 1' and all others (i.e. those who could potentially be 'Type 1').

Of course it's one thing knowing that people may not always choose the most optimal outcomes, and so exist as one of 'Types 2–4' described above, it's another to understand their decision making in such a way that we can close rationality gaps. As Petrarca (2008) urges it is essential that we ensure not only that people know what is right but that we also help people to do the 'right things'. In other words there is no point in social scientists simply disseminating knowledge about ORPs: we must also persuade others to act on this knowledge. A similar view is held by Vico (2002) who argues that common sense (i.e. people's rational choices) must be supported and updated by our increasing understanding of the world. It is clear therefore that as the modern arbiters of virtue or good behaviour[4] social scientists must seek to close the optimal rational gaps by devising interventions to help people to change either their behaviours or beliefs, i.e. to help people make better choices. In the next chapter I begin to explore how we might do so.

## NOTES

1. Often such criticisms have come from previous advocates of RCT. Take for example prominent academic Jon Elster who noted in *Explaining Social Behaviour* (2007, p. 5) that 'I now believe that rational-choice theory has less explanatory power than I used to think. Do real people act on the calculations that make up many pages of mathematical appendixes in leading journals? I do not think so. ... There is no general nonintentional mechanism that can simulate or mimic rationality. ... At the same time, the empirical support ... tends to be quite weak.'

2. I engage with the work of Kant and Aristotle since, while both seminal, their ideas also cohere with many others who recognise the difficulties and tensions involved with fostering virtuous behaviour or excellence (e.g. Plato or Vico).

3. Acting in the collective interest requires a prerequisite notion that we wish to aim for the best group outcomes possible and that we want to use the group's preferences as a guide to action (Rose & Colman, 2007). As such, whether an individual wishes to behave in this way is likely to be related to whether they fully subscribe to the ORP in question.

4. See, e.g. Plato's *Protagoras.*

# CHAPTER 2

# USING SEMIOTIC ANALYSIS TO FILL RATIONALITY GAPS

Key to filling rationality gaps is understanding the relationships that exist between people and things, such as objects and ideas. It is through relationships that things are afforded significance.[1] Correspondingly, it is by examining the nature of the relationships that people have with particular things that enables us to understand the importance these things hold. By way of illustration, when we just examine an object – such as a simple clay pot – in isolation, we can learn a lot about its physical nature, but we learn little about its purpose. Why, for instance, was the pot made? And what is the meaning invested in the pot by its makers or those who own it? By studying the interplay between the pot and those that use it, however, we can understand its significance and role – its place in a given culture.

Each shard of pottery found to date by archaeologists at the Huaca Pucllana excavation site in Lima, for example, have all been adorned with representations of the sea. By studying the customs of the Lima people who populated the site, archaeologists have come to realise the ceremonial purpose of these fragments. Every 20 years the people of the Lima culture would cover over their existing religious and political buildings with earth and build new buildings on top of the old. Pots were created, painted with depictions of their major deity and then ritually smashed as a part of 'closure' ceremonies for the old buildings. It was only by studying these pot remnants in context that their importance and function was revealed. Archaeologists now know that pots at Huaca Pucllana acted as signifiers for regeneration. They were created not for storing corn or produce, but to form the foundation for something new. People from the Lima culture would have seen these pots and intuited their purpose, understanding that the time had come to build upwards once again. Today without that knowledge we may have simply assumed that such pots were for decoration.[2]

Applying the relational approach to ORPs, it seems clear that we will only come to understand people's behaviour in relation to ORPs if we develop a rich understanding of the meaning that an ORP has for people's lives. Furthermore, not only do we need to understand the relationship between people and the ORP itself, but we also need to ascertain the importance and function of alternative actions and beliefs people might pursue. To provide a means to engage in the type of analysis of relationships required by ORP, I turn to semiotics; a theory which holds that all phenomenon and things convey meaning to individuals. As Umberto Eco observes, semiotics is something that is 'concerned with everything that can be *taken* as a sign. A sign is everything which can be taken as significantly substituting for something else' (Eco, 1979, p. 7). A similar view is held by Peirce who suggests that 'a sign is something by knowing we come to know something more' (1934, p. 8.332). In other words, semiotics is concerned with the interpretations that you, I and others associate with words, images, objects or anything else that can be used to signify [indicate] some meaning or other.

Semiotics has a key role to play in relation to ORA because what is signified to us by particular ideas, objects, people and so on is instrumental to how we make choices.[3] In fact, we may think of signification as affecting decision-making in three ways: first, any potential choice will convey to us some indication of the likely benefits given courses of action can provide; second, we also perceive how difficult it is likely to be to pursue different courses of action and finally, different courses of action will convey specific meanings to us. They will also present us with the opportunity to convey particular meaning to others. As Baudrillard (1968) shows, the meaning associated with different choices (what a choice means to us and what it signifies to others) can be a powerful motivator when it comes to how we act as consumers. Here Baudrillard points to the growing power of brands to convey imagery about consumer 'objects' that aren't necessarily inherent within those objects. For instance, holding price and utility constant, often our choices as consumers are a function of whether we find the brand image of a producer appealing and also whether we believe a particular brand's attributes are consistent with, or augment, how we perceive ourselves as individuals, i.e. how they correspond to our own personal brand.

To illustrate how brands can affect consumption I revisit a personal example provided in Brown (2014). The example relates to the period when I had just passed my PhD *viva*. I wanted to make a purchase to mark the occasion and decided to buy a Nespresso coffee maker. At the time the purchase signified to me both the sophistication and status I felt accompanied possessing a doctorate (in addition to acting as an indicator of the taste and eye for design I believed I already possessed). I also felt that the purchase would make a statement about how serious I was about coffee drinking (in itself a signification of my busy, hectic urban life). There were other coffee machines available, but I believed that, for example, a Bialetti stove top espresso maker would not serve as an appropriate marker of my *viva*, whereas a Nespresso Pixie would. To celebrate I wanted 'indulgent' not 'utilitarian' and as noted on the Nespresso website; 'the Nespresso brand stands for exceptional quality, refined service and genuine pleasure. It has become a symbol of elegance'[4] (brand attributes on the Bialetti website meanwhile include 'technological simplicity', 'classic design' and 'enduring quality' – i.e. qualities which flag that their stove top espresso maker is something both original and functional).[5]

The purpose of the example is to illustrate how my interpretation of a particular brand influenced the decision-making process I went through, in essence because I was using the qualities of the brand to signify something about myself (both to myself and to others). But the example also helps illustrate that there is a relationship between brands which affects what and how they signify. Nespresso wouldn't be able to signify luxury or differentiate itself from the idea of more utilitarian coffee makers unless other brands such as Bialetti were positioning themselves as functional and authentic. In other words, a brand invariably signifies what it is by also differentiating itself from what it is not. When viewed from this perspective, consumer choice can be thought of as the process of making sense of the web of signifying relationships that exist between brands as well as situating ourselves within this web. A fundamental aspect of consumption therefore is that we are establishing our own personal brand by positioning it amongst the set of relationships that exist between consumer brands, i.e. we use brands to help signify both who we are and who we are not.

As well as brand, two additional factors will also affect what and how we consume. The first is price. With any given budget, price will determine what we can and cannot actually purchase. This means that our ability to signify through the use of brands is constrained by which brands we can actually afford to buy. The second factor is the utility we perceive a given consumer item can provide. In the example above my assumption was that both Nespresso and Bialetti coffee makers make equally good coffee. More generally, however, different consumer goods of a given type will offer different levels of benefit (e.g. some watches have more functions than others). Typically, there is a direct relationship between benefit and price, with more expensive products tending to enable consumers to do more things or existing things better (although this is not necessarily the case with luxury goods – take, for example, the case of the $300,000 watch that didn't tell the time; Berger, 2016). As a consequence, how we signify and the benefits we can acquire will depend on what our budget will bear.

Although not consumer items in the same way that coffee makers, toasters, jeans or watches are, adherence to ORPs does involve making decisions about how we consume (with the notion of *should* inherent within ORPs replacing the idea of *need* or *want* which typically drives consumption). The examples provided in Chapter 1 require us to drink less alcohol, to eat more fruit and vegetables, to fly less and go to the gym more regularly; each therefore requires us to make choices in terms of how we allocate our resources, be these financial or time-related. As a consequence, in order to act in accordance with a given set of ORPs, we are likely to be required to *spend* more of our food budget in the fruit and vegetable aisle while spending less on wine, spirits and beer. We are likely to have to *spend* more *time* at the gym and less in the air. As with other forms of consumption our finite resources must therefore be allocated appropriately to gain the most well-being from our budget.

As noted earlier, when faced with decisions such as these, what is signified by the choices available to us will be instrumental in how we decide to act. This means that what is crucial to us behaving in accordance with ORPs may be broken down into three things: (1) what the ORP's 'brand' signifies to us, and what we believe engaging with it enables us to signify to others (and how this coheres with the notion of personal brand that I outline in the introduction); (2) the benefits we perceive will result from acting in accordance with an ORP and (3) cost, and whether we can 'afford' to or will find it difficult to act in ways required by the ORP. I now explore these in turn.

*Signification*: Part of the reason we may choose to engage with an ORP is that it reflects who we perceive ourselves to be (i.e. our personal brand). This reflection may represent our current behaviour or behaviour we aspire to. In both cases, however, the ORP's brand is seen as desirable – it represents imagery and attributes that we can connect to and that we want to be associated with.[6] At the same time each of us are multifaceted. We have professional and social aspects of ourselves, we have fashion aspects, we have family aspects, political and cultural aspects, holiday aspects and food aspects: numerous things that when combined make us who we are. This means there is likely to be various intersections between different ORPs and the facets (or brand attributes) of which we are comprised. An ORP related to exercise may, for instance, correspond to an existing facet of the self that views a strict adherence to a four times a week gym routine as a fundamental. Equally it may accord with someone who views a gym routine as aspirational and so something to work towards. It will not resonate remotely, however, with someone who regards going to the gym as a poor way to spend four hours a week that could be better used watching *Netflix*.

At the same time because we are multifaceted and because these different facets appear as more or less relevant in different situations, we can face tensions in terms of what we wish to signify at particular points in time. We may indeed view exercise as aspirational but equally we may wish to associate ourselves with drinking late into the night in Copenhagen's meat packing district. We may not only connect with the ideals of Turin's 'Slow Food' movement, but also relate to the 'dirty satisfaction' of fast burgers and shakes of Southampton's 7bone. To reduce our carbon footprint we may identify with the imagery of catching the sleeper train from Paris, but the lure of a trip to Machu Picchu may also resonate with a more adventurous aspect of the self. The implications for ORPs are that their 'brand' needs to be not only attractive enough for people to want to engage, but also so appealing that we are dissuaded from seeking out alternatives (or at least dissuaded from seeking out alternatives as frequently as we currently do). In other words, to achieve optimal rational outcomes, ORPs require us to become brand loyal: to want to associate enough with what the ORP stands for that we more often than not eschew other options.

*Benefits*: ORPs also need to clearly signify their benefits to enable us to choose between the ORP and other attractive options. The benefits of attending the gym or eating healthy are generally self-apparent and tangible; doing these things will make us fitter and healthier, they will enable us to live longer and they reduce the risks of us suffering from heart disease and cancer, of developing Type 2 diabetes and of becoming obese. The benefits of other types of ORP are perhaps less apparent; for example, how should an individual conceive of the immediate benefits to themselves of recycling or cutting their carbon emissions? Because the benefits of certain ORPs tend to be less personally tangible in nature they require us to consider impacts that reside beyond the immediate self and instead serve the good of the long-term collective. This is hard for people to do and easy for them to ignore. One way to encourage people to consider impacts in this way, however, is to connect intangible benefits to the signification associated with the ORP. We may not be able to immediately touch or feel the impact of (for example) recycling, but we can be recognised and socially appreciated – or afforded kudos – for behaving in more environmentally friendly ways. Again therefore the attractiveness of the ORP's brand needs to incorporate within it a way of socially acknowledging and differentiating between those that engage and act in accordance with an ORP and those that do not.

*Costs*: Finally, ORPs need to signify their costs to ensure individuals understand what is required to engage with them. With some ORPs costs will involve an element of price: we can establish how much a monthly gym membership costs and so ascertain how to incorporate this into our budget. Likewise, it is easy to find out the cost of using public transport compared to cars or the price of purchasing particular types of food. With many ORPs, however, there are non-financial costs that need to be considered. Such non-financial costs include the time it takes to engage in a particular type of activity. Getting a train to and from Venice, for instance – which at its fastest takes around 15 hours one way – effectively rules out this approach for a weekend break; going for a 30-minute stroll, however, can take place in one's lunch hour. There is also the cost of perceived effort, which affects how hard we think it will be to access particular benefits. For example, one of the most common reasons given for eating fast food is taste.[7] Taste is also the reason many give for not eating vegetables.[8] Yet prepared in the right way vegetables are extremely tasty; undertaking such preparation, however, takes time and effort. Our perceptions of what is required will therefore directly impact on whether we are willing to undertake this preparation. On occasions we may lack knowledge of the costs involved with an ORP, which can also affect the choices we make. When in Copenhagen I was keen to hire and ride a bike from my hotel and the conference I was attending. What stopped me was that I was unsure of how to hire a bike, what the rules of the road were in Denmark and where I would leave the bike while in seminars. This lack of information made hiring a bike too costly – I felt exposed to number of potential 'risks', ranging from sustaining an accident to having the bike stolen. There was also the potential for social embarrassment since I dreaded the idea of having to admit my ignorance of these things to someone at some point.

In the last chapter I illustrated how we can differentiate between individuals according to their attitudes and behaviours towards given ORPs. While useful for highlighting the existence of rationality gaps and their type (i.e. Types 2–4), closing these gaps requires something more. In this chapter I have argued that when faced with choices, our decisions based on a combination of the meaning, usefulness and costs we perceive are signified by the options available. In essence these three signifying factors may be considered as the well-being that is gained from making specific decisions. Adding this semiotic approach to the matrix established in the last chapter now provides a framework that can be used to develop a more in-depth understanding of why people respond to ORPs in different ways. By exploring what is signified to different people when they consider ORPs we can begin to understand the essential variations in their perceptions of meaning, usefulness and cost: why an ORP can be seen as attractive, useful and easy to attain to one set of individuals and not to another. Furthermore, why individuals may prefer to choose alternatives to the ORP. This is illustrated in Figure 2.1. We can also begin to develop ideas for how to alter what is signified in order to increase perceived well-being and so the likelihood that people will engage with the ORP. A good place to start is by exploring what is signified to those who are categorised as Type 1 and those categorised as Types 2–4. This will enable us to ascertain the essential differences in signification that occur between those who are currently fully engaged in an ORP and those who are not. From here we can then look for clues as to the types of interventions we might develop to reduce such differences.

I finish the chapter by noting that the analysis above is designed to convey what happens during processes of 'active' decision-making. Active decisions require us to consciously consider specific information – such as the requirements of a new ORP – and in doing so we become conscious of what this information signifies to us. Once a decision has been made, however (e.g. we decide to engage with the ORP), and we begin to incorporate this decision into our everyday lives, the conscious signification associated with that decision begins to diminish. This is because we are no longer actively considering the choice but enacting it. While we may still refer to the signification in the early stages of enactment as a means of reinforcing why we are doing what we are doing, after a while what was previously a new action becomes habit. The habitualisation of the decision, in effect, serves to subsume what was previously a conscious signification into our multifaceted self. In other words, decisions to engage in activity such as eating

**Figure 2.1. Incorporating Semiotic Analysis into the OR Matrix.**

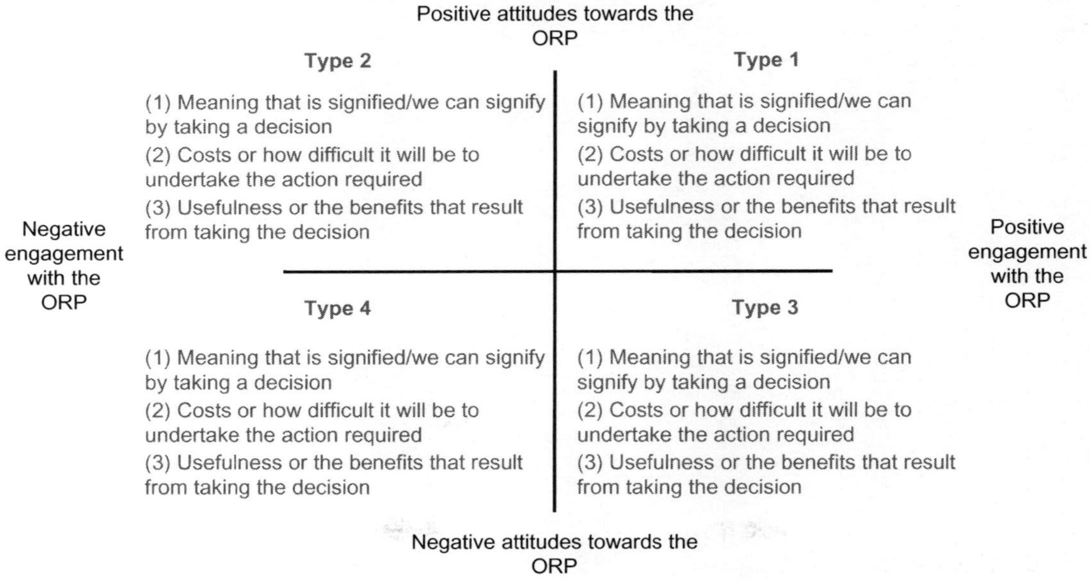

Positive attitudes towards the ORP

|  | Type 1 | Positive engagement with the ORP |
|---|---|---|
| **Type 2** | | |
| (1) Meaning that is signified/we can signify by taking a decision | (1) Meaning that is signified/we can signify by taking a decision | |
| (2) Costs or how difficult it will be to undertake the action required | (2) Costs or how difficult it will be to undertake the action required | |
| (3) Usefulness or the benefits that result from taking the decision | (3) Usefulness or the benefits that result from taking the decision | |
| **Type 4** | **Type 3** | |
| (1) Meaning that is signified/we can signify by taking a decision | (1) Meaning that is signified/we can signify by taking a decision | |
| (2) Costs or how difficult it will be to undertake the action required | (2) Costs or how difficult it will be to undertake the action required | |
| (3) Usefulness or the benefits that result from taking the decision | (3) Usefulness or the benefits that result from taking the decision | |

Negative engagement with the ORP

Negative attitudes towards the ORP

'five a day' and cycling to work, running in the evening and cutting down on CFCs simply become part of who we are (and so part of our brand and what we signify). We are only likely to consciously return to this signification when faced with decisions that put the various aspects of our multifaceted self on a collision course with one other, or when we experience needs or situations that disrupt us from the habits we are in. For example, when we have embraced healthy eating and exercise but also really feel like a greasy burger. Here we must find ways to moderate between these things and balance the well-being (i.e. the meaning, usefulness and cost) that each accords us: for instance, we may decide that a suitable balance is to enjoy the occasional burger but to make sure that when we do we increase our gym routine to compensate; in another situation we may take a long-haul flight but then leave the car at home for the everyday work commute. Again the more attractive the ORP's brand and the more well-being we are perceived to gain from it the more likely, in the face of such conflicts, needs or disruptions, that our decisions will result in, or come as close as possible to, outcomes that are optimal rational.

## NOTES

1. This position was first put forward by Italian political philosopher Vico in his 1725 book *The New Science* (*Principi di Scienza Nuova d'intorno alla Comune Natura delle Nazioni*). Vico's suggestion was that individuals and groups not only construct the social world through action and interaction but also perceive 'truths' about objects, ideas and other people (Vico, 2002). In turn these truths begin to structure the relationships that

individuals and groups have with those objects, ideas and people and so influence how the social world is constructed moving forwards. Criticising what he saw as the reductionism of the enlightenment, Vico argued that the development of the then nascent notion of social science should privilege not the study of independently existing phenomenon (as the natural sciences proposed), but rather the study of relationships that exist between people and objects, ideas and other people. This is because every element in a given situation has no significance by itself − its significance is determined by its relationships to all other elements involved within a situation (Hawkes, 1978, p. 18). Similar ideas were later adopted by the Swiss linguist Saussure in *Cours de Linguistique Générale* where it is argued that when studying language we should not just simply examine individual words but the relationships between words within a wider system, with these relationships serving to ensure the words can work together to create meaning. An analogous perspective is also put forward by Umberto Eco when considering translation. Here Eco argues that when the translation of a text is attempted on a word-by-word basis, the result, when read in its entirety, typically fails to fully capture the author's original meaning (Eco, 2003). Instead effective translation focuses less on stand-alone words and more on what the author intended. In other words effective translation examines the role each word was playing as part of an structure designed to convey meaning.

2. See: http://huacapucllanamiraflores.pe

3. Understanding how we make choices is widely regarded as key to understanding how we might enact behavioural change (see, e.g. Elster, 2007).

4. See: https://www.nestle-nespresso.com/about-us/strategy/creating-long-lasting-consumer-relationships

5. See: http://www.bialetti.com/coffee/stovetop/moka-express-c-1_7_22.html

6. Desirability in this sense could also include social duty since it can be attractive for people to know that they are doing 'something good' or 'the right thing to do'.

7. See: http://www.webmd.com/food-recipes/news/20081202/top-11-reasons-for-fast-foods-popularity

8. See: https://www.diet-blog.com/07/5_reasons_why_we_dont_eat_healthy_food.php

# CHAPTER 3

# A CASE STUDY FROM
# EDUCATION – PART 1

In the preceding chapters I established the notion of optimal rational positions, I presented the concept of optimal rationality as a means to explain people's behaviour and I introduced semiotics as a way to understand what might enable us to change that behaviour in order to achieve more optimal outcomes. In this chapter and in Chapter 4, I present an example of this optimal rational/semiotic (ORS) approach in action, drawing on a case study from education. Specifically I use the next two chapters to examine how the ORS framework was employed to develop and implement an initiative designed to encourage teachers to engage in *evidence-informed* practices.

To provide some context for the case study, across many countries, national and district level governments are increasingly pursuing approaches to school improvement that seek to achieve so-called 'bottom-up' change (i.e. starting from the level of the individual teacher) (Brown, Schildkamp, & Hubers, 2017). In particular, educational 'self-improvement' is now viewed by many as *the* preferred approach to enhancing provision at the school and system level (Greany, 2015). At the same time, the economic imperative to reduce national debt levels following the global financial crisis of the last decade means that many education systems, including those across Europe, are experiencing a decrease in financial support (Brown et al., 2017; Greany, 2015). As a result of the drive for self-improvement and the decline in funding for top-down mandates, teachers and schools are now required to develop the capacity to: (1) identify core problems in relation to teaching and learning; (2) discover the causes underpinning these problems and (3) design and implement appropriate actions for improving student outcomes.

An approach often turned to by schools facing such challenges is that of evidence-informed practice (EIP). This approach involves fostering situations in which teaching practice is consciously informed by knowledge such as: (1) formal research produced by researchers; (2) evidence derived from practitioner inquiry and/or (3) evidence derived from routinely collected school or system-level data (e.g. pupil assessment data; Cain, 2015; Galdin-O'Shea, 2015; Nutley, Walter, & Davies, 2002). While EIP in education tends to be broadly defined, typically teachers, schools and school systems attempt to achieve EIP via approaches that are much narrower in focus. In particular, for the purposes of this book, I concentrate on EIP involving the collaborative use of existing research evidence by teachers so that they might design and implement interventions that can achieve positive change across their schools.

In the Introduction I suggested that ORPs emerge as a result of: (1) a robust and credible evidence base in relation to current or potential new behaviours; (2) a well-reasoned argument (or theory of change) which provides this evidence with meaning; (3) a social, moral or value-based imperative setting out the need for change based on this meaning and

(4) buy-in to this imperative from a range of credible stakeholders. Correspondingly that EIP can be considered an ORP emerges as a result of the following four steps.

Collaborative EIP can have positive benefits for both teachers and students (Step 1). For example, correlational data reported by Mincu (2014) suggest that where research is used as part of high-quality initial teacher education and ongoing professional development, it is associated with higher teacher, school and system performance (similar relationships are also reported in Sebba, Tregenza, & Kent, 2012; Godfrey, 2014, 2016). More recently Rose and colleagues (2017), using a randomised control trial across a sample of 119 schools, showed that increased levels of collaborative research-use by primary school teachers had a significant impact on primary school student's exam results. CUREE (2010), meanwhile, lists a range of positive teacher outcomes that emerge from collaborative EIP including both improvements in pedagogic knowledge and skills, and greater teacher confidence. Furthermore, the experience of 'research-engaged' schools that take a strategic and concerted approach in this area appear to be positive, with studies suggesting that research engagement can shift school behaviours from a superficial 'hints and tips' model of improvement to a learning culture in which staff work together to understand what appears to work, when and why (Godfrey, 2016; Handscomb & MacBeath, 2003).

A theory of change for why EIP should improve teaching and student outcomes is set out in Brown et al. (2017) (Step 2). Broadly this argues that there is a multitude of research that currently exists that can help teachers in a number of areas of their work. For example, research can be used to: (1) aid teachers in the design of new bespoke strategies for teaching and learning in order to tackle specific identified problems; (2) provide teachers with ideas for how to improve aspects of their day-to-day practice by drawing on approaches that research has shown to be effective; (3) help teachers expand, clarify and deepen their own concepts, including the concepts they use to understand students, curriculum and teaching practice and (4) provide teachers with specific programs or guidelines, shown by research to be effective, which set out how to engage in various aspects of teaching or specific approaches to improve learning. Thus, if teachers are able to engage with this research in a way that enables them to undertake any of (1)–(4) above, their teaching quality should be improved. Correspondingly, improved teaching quality should then lead to improved student outcomes. To engage effectively with research, however, will require teachers to be able to: (1) access research; (2) make sense of research findings and relate these to their specific context or problem area; (3) where relevant, develop and implement a research-informed intervention and (4) gauge the effectiveness of their efforts and amend their course of action based on the impact they are having.

Given that it is possible to use research evidence to improving teaching practices then teachers *should* engage in EIP (Step 3). This imperative stems from advocates such as Oakley, who argues that evidence-informed approaches ensure that 'those who intervene in other people's lives do so with the utmost benefit and least harm' (2000, p. 3); also described by Alton-Lee (2012) as the 'first do no harm' principle. Oakley thus contends that there exists a moral imperative for practitioners to only make decisions, or to take action, when armed with the best available evidence. In other words that: 'we [all] share an interest in being able to live our lives as well as we can, free from ill-informed intervention and in the best knowledge we can gather of what is likely to make all of us most healthy, most productive, most happy and most able to contribute to the common good' (2000, p. 323). More recently Goldacre (2013) also argued that teachers *should* engage in EIP since it would lead not only to improved outcomes for children but also increased professional independence (resulting in teaching experiencing an 'enhanced' level of professionalisation akin to that of doctors). Likewise England's Chartered College of Teaching recently suggested that teachers' engagement with research should be viewed as the hallmark of an effective profession.[1]

It is evident that there now exists a general position in favour of teachers pursing collaborative EIP (Step 4). For instance, the direction of travel of recent educational policy in England and elsewhere (including, e.g. Australia, Netherlands, Norway, Ontario, United States) focuses strongly on promoting, assisting and requiring teachers to better engage with research (Coldwell et al., 2017; Stoll, 2015; Whitty & Wisby, 2017). It is also apparent from recent announcements by organisations, such as the Education Endowment Foundation (EEF), who in 2014 launched a £1.4m fund to improve the use of research in schools (EEF, 2014) and in 2016 launched the *Research Schools* initiative.[2] In addition, this position can be associated with the rise of bottom-up/teacher-led initiatives, such as the emerging network of 'Teachmeets'[3] and 'ResearchED'[4] conferences (Galdin-O'Shea, 2015; Whitty & Wisby, 2017) designed to help teachers connect more effectively with educational research. One recent prominent example of such teacher-led initiatives was the 2017 launch of England's Chartered College of Teaching: an organisation led by and for teachers in order to support the use of EIP (Whitty & Wisby, 2017). Finally, this position is also reflected in a recent content analysis of the websites and school policy documents of 100 teaching schools (Coldwell et al., 2017), which shows how the majority claim both to be promoting research-use and having mechanisms in place to ensure the collaborative engagement by teachers with educational research.

*The Chestnut Church of England Learning Federation*: The case that forms the focus of the analysis in this chapter is that of the Chestnut Church of England Learning Federation; a family of three small church infant schools based in the Hampshire villages of Rosebush, All Saints and Southampton Common. These three schools all work closely together under the leadership of the Federation principal and Governing Body and share a vision of ensuring children grow up to lead safe, happy, healthy and successful lives by benefitting from the highest standard of education and the opportunity for each child to attain their own, full potential.

One of the Federation's improvement plan objectives for the academic year 2016–2017 was for it to become an evidence-informed Federation where teachers and schools collaborate to rigorously evaluate the quality of the education they offer, understand what they need to do to improve, to take appropriate evidence-informed action and to evaluate the impact of their actions, enabling them to achieve together. To meet this objective, the Executive principal proposed a school improvement plan to move school professional development in the Federation away from traditional professional development models and towards one in which all teachers are engaged in evidence-informed enquiry. In particular, the aim of Chestnut Learning Federation's model for evidence-use was to achieve the following goals:

- that teachers are able to engage with external research to identify potential pedagogic innovations that can improve teaching and learning within the Federation;

- that teachers are able to use evidence-informed enquiry to trial and evaluate the impact of new approaches to teaching and learning;

- that teachers operate in an effective learning environment that facilitates the sharing of best practice and

- that teachers are facilitated to work collaboratively so that impactful innovations and effective pedagogic practices are modelled and embedded across all three schools.

This chapter uses the ORS approach to explore the context for the roll out of the evidence-informed school improvement model developed by Chestnut Learning Federation, and to show what the ORS approach indicates was needed for the Federation to move towards the ORP of EIP. The research questions addressed by the ORS approach were in terms of the Chestnut Learning Federation model of evidence-informed improvement:

1. What are the pre-intervention perceptions of staff in relation to collaborative EIP?

2. What is the signification initially associated with EIP within the Chestnut Learning Federation?

3. What might be required to shift the current signification associated with evidence-use within Chestnut Learning Federation towards that of the ORP of EIP?

To address these questions a qualitative methodology was employed. For research question (1) in-depth semi-structured interviews were used to collect pre-intervention data on the attitudes towards and engagement in EIP by Chestnut's staff. Data were collected using measures based on a study into research-use amongst 696 primary schools teachers in England undertaken by Brown and Zhang (2016); these

---

### Table 3.1. Measures of Research-use from Brown and Zhang (2016).

(1) Information from research plays an important role in informing my teaching practice.

(2) I have found information from research useful in applying new approaches in the classroom.

(3) I do not support implementing a school-wide change without research to support it.

(4) I do not support implementing a Federation-wide change without research to support it.

(5) In the last year, I have discussed relevant research findings with colleagues in my school.

(6) In the last year, I have discussed relevant research findings with colleagues in the Federation.

---

measures are set out in Table 3.1. The qualitative versions of these questions, however, invited exploration rather than seek to replicate Brown and Zhang's measure of agreement using Likert scales.

For research questions (2) and (3) questions were developed in relation to the three factors signified to us when we are required to make choices concerning an ORP. These are: (1) what the ORP's 'brand' means to us, and what we believe engaging with it enables us to signify to others (sample question: 'When I say evidence-informed teaching, what image does that convey to you?'); (2) the benefits we perceive will result from acting in accordance with an ORP (sample question: 'in terms of ways of improving practice, how effective is using research evidence? Why?') and (3) cost, and whether we can 'afford' to, or will find it difficult to act in ways required by the ORP (sample question: 'In terms of ways of improving practice, how "costly" is using evidence? Prompt

**Table 3.2. Characteristics of the Interview Respondents.**

| Gender | 14 Female (93%), 1 Male (7%) |
| --- | --- |
| Average time in post | 9 years |
| Average age bracket | 46–50 |
| Number with post-graduate qualifications | 5 (38%) |
| Middle or senior leaders | 6 (46%) |

in terms of time, money, training, etc.'). Questions were also asked in relation to the background, values and beliefs of respondents.

A total of 15 teachers were interviewed in September 2016 (representing the whole of the Federation's teaching staff). The characteristics of the respondents are set out in Table 3.2. Interviews were recorded and these recordings transcribed. Data from the recordings were analysed thematically, first to ascertain the OR *type* of participants and then to ascertain their perspectives in relation to the three signifying factors above.

Beginning with the analysis of the OR *type* of participants, here type was determined by looking at teachers' responses to questions (1) and (4) in Table 3.1. In other words by examining teachers' beliefs as to whether they subscribe to the notion of EIP driving Federation level changes to teaching and learning and whether they themselves engage in EIP to improve teaching and learning. It can be seen in Figure 3.1 that there was a fairly wide distribution of respondents according to whether they believed they used research to improve their practice (or not) – question (1) in Table 3.1 AND/OR whether respondents were in favour of a school or

**Figure 3.1.** Allocation of Respondents According to OR Type.

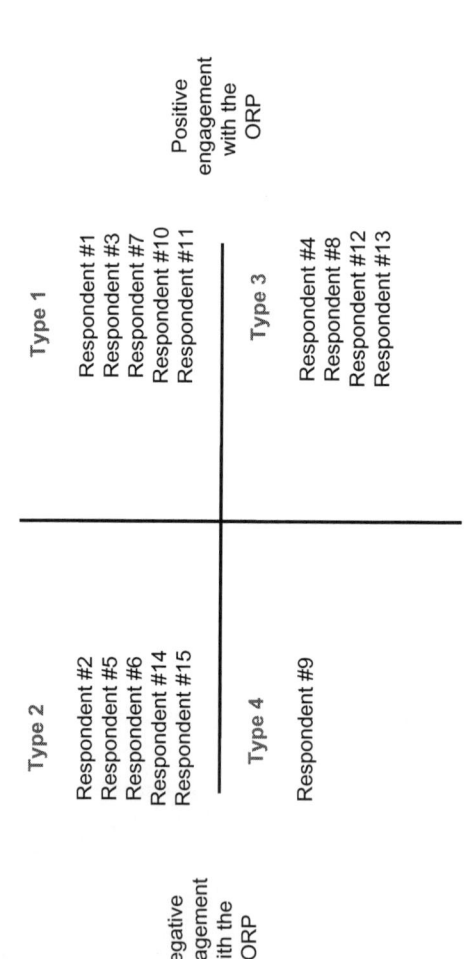

federation level commitment to using research to improve practice (or not) – question (4) in Table 3.1. Overall a third of respondents indicated they believed in and acted in accordance with the ORP (i.e. were 'Type 1'). The remaining two-thirds were predominantly Types '2' and '3', although one respondent was an out and out rejecter of the ORP ('Type 4'). Overall within the Federation there was sizable rationality gap of 66%.

Following this initial allocation of participants, thematic analysis was subsequently employed to identify all germane perceptions or perspectives from the interview data in terms of the signification (meaning), benefits and costs associated with EIP. Specifically a hierarchy of thematic codes was developed to explain interview responses, with the development of codes occurring both inductively and deductively (Lincoln & Guba, 1985): inductive analysis was first used to provide an initial categorisation of responses, and once all data were coded this way, mid-level codes were built from the aggregation of these codes until all of the initial codes could be adequately explained in a conceptually meaningful way. These mid-level codes were then organised within the higher level codes of benefits, cost and signifying values (BCS values). The resulting coding tree is set out in Figure 3.2, and the allocation of codes by quadrant is set out in Figure 3.3.

Following coding, a comparison was then made between the codes sitting under each BCS value domain within each quadrant. This was done in order to ascertain whether there were any meaningful differences in respondents' semiotic perspectives vis-à-vis their differing ORP *types*. A full analysis of the interview findings can be found in Appendix at the end of this book. For brevity, in this chapter I have provided a summary of the main findings.

**Figure 3.2. The Hierarchy of Thematic Codes.**

| Benefits | Cost | Signifying |
|---|---|---|
| Recognises the benefits of using research | Time<br>• competing priorities<br>• time to do it right<br>  – making time<br>• sharing with colleagues<br>  – making time | Reflective, empowered teachers who constantly improve their practice |
| Recognises school or federation support for EIP | | Confidence to collaborate |
| Enquiry mindset<br>• reflection on academic research<br>• felt able to experiment<br>• how to experiment<br>• confidence | | Providing a route to better practice |
| | Financial cost | Useful tool which provides a route to better student outcomes |
| Collaborative orientation<br>• learning conversations | Access | Confident professional autonomy |
| Network orientation<br>• networked learning conversations<br>• knew who to turn to for support<br>• Knew where to go to access research | | Performativity and accountability |

*Type 1*: Beginning with the *benefits* that were signified by EIP, five mid-level and nine initial codes were identified within the Type 1 quadrant. The first of these mid-level codes was *recognises the benefits of using research*, which highlights respondents' beliefs that the regular use of research to inform practice would result in better outcomes for children. Responses within the Type 1 quadrant also highlighted that this group knew how to maximise the *benefits* of EIP. For example, they displayed an *enquiry mindset* illustrating they *felt able to experiment* with research *and* that they knew *how to experiment* with research, thus meaning they were happy to trial new approaches to teaching and learning. Participants engaged in *learning conversations* as a way of assessing whether and how new EIP should be adopted. Furthermore, participants also displayed a *network orientation* in that they

**Figure 3.3.**   **Allocation of Thematic Codes According to Respondent's ORP Type.**

Positive attitudes towards the
ORP

|  | Positive engagement with the ORP |
| --- | --- |
| **Negative engagement with the ORP** | |

**Benefits**
- Recognises school or federation support for EIP
- (+ve) Enquiry mindset
- (+ve) Collaborative orientation
- (+ve) Network orientation

**Cost**
- Time – 3 sub-categories
- Access

**Signifying**
- Providing a route to better practice
- Confidence to collaborate

**Benefits**
- Recognises the benefits of using research
- Recognises school or federation support for EIP
- (+ve) Enquiry mindset – 3 sub-categories
- (+ve) Collaborative orientation
- (+ve) Network orientation – 3 sub-categories

**Cost**
- Time – 2 sub-categories
- Financial cost

**Signifying**
- Reflective, empowered teachers who constantly improve their practice
- Confidence to collaborate

**Benefits**
- Cynicism
- (?) Valued activity
- (-ve) Enquiry mindset

**Cost**
- Time
- Access

**Signifying**
- Performativity and accountability

**Benefits**
- Recognises the benefits of using research
- (+ve) Recognises school or federation support for EIP
- (+ve) Enquiry mindset – 2 sub-categories
- (local) Purpose
- (-ve) Network orientation

**Cost**
- Time

**Signifying**
- Useful tool which provides a route to better student outcomes
- Confident professional autonomy

Negative attitudes towards the
ORP

*knew who to turn to for support*, i.e. that they were able to identify who within the federation might support them with engaging in EIP if required. Also that respondents *knew where to go to access research*, i.e. they could identify who and where they might go to access research.

Moving to the *cost* value, two mid-level codes were identified. The first of these was *time*, which was often regarded as a barrier to achieving even more (with the initial level coding reflecting the need to find *time to do it right*). Included here was the time needed to ensure that sufficient good quality research could be drawn on. *Sharing with colleagues* or the brokerage of research or research-informed strategies was also seen as key but time consuming, since it was recognised that sharing is only effective when research is 'effectively translated'. Finally, in terms of the *signifying* values of EIP, respondents suggested that, to them, EIP signalled the presence of *reflective, empowered teachers who constantly improve their practice*. At the same time, findings here also suggest that respondents viewed the use of research as something that would provide the *confidence to collaborate* with others across the federation: the use of research thus seen as providing a firm basis upon which to debate and engage in discussion around effective forms of teaching and learning.

*Type 2*: Moving now to the Type 2 quadrant and beginning again with the *benefits*, four mid-level and initial codes were identified. In all cases the benefits related to how EIP could augment teachers' existing practices. For example, participants already *felt able to experiment*; thus teachers could see how research could strengthen this process. As with the Type 1 quadrant, *learning conversations* (reflecting participant's *collaborative orientation*) were often used and seen as a beneficial way of challenging entrenched practice that might not always be effective: learning conversations were thus seen as something that could be potentially strengthened by research. Respondents in this quadrant also actively connected with colleagues in other schools in order to collaborate and learn from each other through *networked learning conversations* (again reflecting their *network orientation*) and again saw how research could augment such conversations.

Four mid-level codes were identified for *cost*, of these three were related to the time costs associated with engaging in EIP. For this quadrant, such costs were associated with the *time [needed] to do it right*, i.e. engaging with research effectively and meaningfully. What's more, the cost of time also stretched to *sharing with colleagues:* ensuring that colleagues, such as teaching assistants (TA) understood how to use the approach as well. In both cases there was an anxiety about finding this time (*making time*), but it was felt that such issues would be manageable if protected time was allocated. One final cost value code was the cost of *access*. Here some expressed a worry as to whether they might understand formal academic research.

In terms of the *signifying* values, it was clear that respondents in this quadrant associated EIP with the qualities of the *enquiry mindset* expressed by others those already engaged in research-use (i.e. those in quadrants Types 1 and 3) with that mindset then *providing a route to better practice*. More specifically, EIP was associated with teachers who reflect using research and develop deeper pedagogic knowledge as a result; who are willing to try new approaches; who experiment to take risks to improve practice. What's more, research-use was also seen to provide *confidence to collaborate* and a secure basis for evidence-informed teachers to be both collaborative and network orientated.

*Type 3*: Within the Type 3 quadrant there were five *benefit* codes, one *cost* code and one *signifying* code. In contrast to the first two quadrants, however, two of the *benefit* codes indicated negative perspectives and a further use code represented a localised focus. The first of the positive benefit codes was *recognises the benefits of using research*. In other words, it was thought by respondents in this quadrant that using research could result in better practice. Others noted that because they had just taught a difficult cohort of children, they had turned to research to provide them with specific pedagogic strategies. It was also apparent that respondents within this quadrant exhibited an *enquiry mindset*. This was indicated first by participants' *reflection on academic research*. Here, as before, this code often applied to the responses of those who had relatively recently completed a degree, or post-graduate qualification.

In terms of the negative codes, it was clear that participants in this quadrant could *not* point to examples of leadership support directed at encouraging EIP more widely (*recognises school/federation level of support for EIP*). This meant that this group did not tend to experiment and further stressed that the focus of the research-use activity needed a recognisable purpose if they were to buy into it. Sometimes this meant that they felt the locus for EIP should be at the level of the classroom rather than the level of the federation.

What's more, the *network orientation* of participants indicated a lack of depth of engagement with others. While those in the Type 1 and Type 2 quadrants employed *networked learning conversations*, those in this quadrant were more likely to engage in more superficial collaboration with networked peers. For example, the simple sharing (i.e. cost) of resource, rather than deep engagement with peers that centres on how to use the resource effectively. Finally, a key issue for those in this quadrant was the number of *competing priorities* that often seemed to 'get in the way' of research-use (the cost vale of *time*). With these factors combined, it is per-haps no surprise that when it came to the *signifying* values associated with research-use, respondents within this quad-rant tended to articulate a practical purpose. For instance, evidence-use was regarded as a *useful tool* which *provides a route to better student outcomes*. A research-informed teacher meanwhile was seen as having good pedagogic knowledge: research-use thus seen as providing the basis for *confident professional autonomy*. In keeping with the analy-sis above, the imagery associated with EIP also had a local focus that involved teachers operating in their classrooms in their own way.

*Type 4*: Only one respondent provided responses to suggest that they held Type 4 beliefs. Although these responses were atypical in comparison to those held by other respon-dents, it is possible to triangulate these codes to the analy-sis above. Doing so shows that in terms of *benefit*, unlike with other quadrants, this participant did not *feel able to experiment* (they thus demonstrated a negative *enquiry mindset*). In terms of *cost* value, this respondent also flagged the issue of *competing priorities*. Finally, while respondents located in the other three quadrants univer-sally linked EIP to solving problems, developing an enquiry habit of mind (OECD, 2016), becoming a reflective practi-tioner and developing twenty-first-century learners, this respondent linked EIP directly to *performativity and accountability*.

Having established an understanding of the various per-spectives that exist regarding collaborative EIP, the next step was to develop an intervention to increase Type 1 beliefs and behaviours. This process for doing so is described in the next chapter.

## NOTES

1. See: https://chartered.college/chartered-teacher-professional-principles

2. See: https://educationendowmentfoundation.org.uk/our-work/research-schools/

3. See: http://www.teachmeethants.co.uk/sample-page/

4. See: http://www.workingoutwhatworks.com

# CHAPTER 4

# A CASE STUDY FROM
# EDUCATION – PART 2

In the last chapter I showed how, through analysing ORS interview data, we could examine people's perspectives and behaviours in relation to a given ORP (in this case, collaborative EIP). Doing so meant it was possible to examine why people belonged to specific rationality types and so why their behaviour was or wasn't optimal in nature. Building on from this initial work, I now use this chapter to show how it is possible to develop interventions, grounded in the understanding that emerges from this initial analysis, to shift individuals' beliefs and actions, thus enabling them to become more optimally rational. In other words, develop interventions that move individuals towards the beliefs and behaviours of the Type 1 quadrant. I begin this process by exploring what the earlier 'pre-intervention' interview data revealed in terms of the factors preventing individuals from acting in an optimally rational way.

The analysis undertaken in Chapter 3 (a fuller version of the analysis can be found in the appendix) suggests that a number of perceived *cost* and *benefit* factors were contributing to teachers behaving in less than optimal ways in relation to collaborative EIP. These include a lack of opportunities to engage with research evidence and so a dearth of experience in terms of the benefits of using research evidence to improve practice (Type 2 respondents); a lack of access to research (Type 2 and some Type 3 respondents); respondents worrying whether they would be able to understand research evidence (Type 2 respondents); concerns such as having enough time to engage effectively with research evidence or having time to show others how to engage with evidence-informed interventions (Types 2 and 3 respondents); and worries regarding *how* to engage with research evidence and whether they would engage in the 'right' way (Types 2 and 4 respondents). Some respondents also viewed EIP as a localised and reactive activity, rather than something that could be used collaboratively and proactively to drive continuous improvement (Type 3 respondents).

In addition, a number of *benefit-* and *signifying*-related factors also contributed to respondents holding less than optimal beliefs regarding EIP. For instance, there were concerns that not engaging 'properly' with research evidence would have professional consequences; meaning EIP as a concept was rejected because of its perceived relationship to performitivity (this was exemplified by the Type 4 respondent's perception that they were currently 'not allowed' to experiment to improve classroom practice). In some cases, respondents also believed that there was little benefit in engaging in wider collaborative endeavours in relation to EIP or that the competing priorities they faced meant that such collaboration was not possible (Types 3 and 4 respondents); also that these kinds of collaborative endeavours would not be supported by the Chestnut Learning Federation's school leadership team (Types 3 and 4 respondents).

At the same time, looking across the responses of those who did use research in some form or other (i.e. Types 1 and 3 respondents), it could be seen that participant's first-hand understanding of the benefits of using research was key to driving *actual engagement with research evidence*. Often these individuals had had recent formal experience of *reflection on academic research*, possibly via postgraduate study. A key driver of respondents' positive attitudes towards EIP meanwhile (irrespective of whether they were Type 1 or 2) was that EIP was seen as representing a community-wide endeavour: in this respect, EIP was viewed as representing a culture rather than an activity, since it involves schools engaging with research to focus on strategic as well as local priorities (Stoll, Bolam, McMahon, Wallace, & Thomas, 2006). It would seem, therefore, that a fundamental part of what drives optimal attitudes towards collaborative EIP is the extent to which research use is perceived as being something that should extend beyond the local setting. That is, optimal attitudes towards EIP relate to both respondents' *collaborative* and *networked* orientations (e.g. their use of learning conversations and networked learning conversations) and the extent to which evidence-use signifies not just a tool, but something that leads to twenty-first-century teaching and learning within what the OECD refers to as 'learning organisations' (OECD, 2016). Alongside this is the recognition from teachers that senior leaders within the federation are encouraging the EIP agenda (*recognises school/federation level of support for EIP)* and, vitally, that leaders also engaging in acts (such as timetabling) to enable networked collaboration.

In order to address these factors and meet the aims of Chestnut Learning Federation's school improvement plan, a form of Research Learning Community (RLC) approach was developed for the Federation's teachers. The aim of the RLC was to facilitate EIP within the Federation by shifting the attitudes and behaviours of type 2–4 teachers such that they cohered with those teachers within the Federation already identified as Type 1 (in other words, those who already believed that the collaborative EIP represented the right thing to do and also engaged in it). The key attributes of the RLC included:

1. a cycle of enquiry approach involving four, one day workshops (with the time for all teachers to attend the workshops made available and protected). In these workshops a structured approach supported teachers to: engage with and reflect on academic research; develop interventions informed by this research which could be trialled and refined; and help to assess the impact and the benefits that accrued from these research-informed interventions;

2. the provision of easily accessible (i.e. understandable) research evidence and exercises that enabled teachers to relate the research to their current practices and contexts;

3. the development of a learning community culture which: explicitly valued the importance of collegiality; fostered trust; welcomed diverse perspectives; enabled mutual learning (i.e. both individual learning and learning for the Federation as a whole); established that all teachers in the Federation were responsible for the learning of every child in the Federation (whether children belonged to their class or not); and encouraged warranted risk taking in the development of new teaching practices. Alongside this was an explicit acknowledgement by Federation leaders that new EIPs might not always work first time (and the reassurance by leaders that this was ok).

In addition, pre-intervention interview data suggested the notion of collaborative evidence-informed professional development was linked by some Type 1 individuals to the Finnish model of teaching and learning.[1] To them, the Finnish model signified professionalisation, the absence of performativity and top-down mandate, but at the same time high educational achievement (in part due to Finland's traditionally good standing in international tests of education performance). Recognising that the Finnish model might prove an attractive signifying hook, its key facets were summarised and presented to those who were rejecters of EIP. This group too found it exciting and attractive, as did Types 2 and 3 individuals. Because the Finnish model proved generally compelling, key aspects of the approach developed for Chestnut were subsequently linked to it throughout the year-long process. In other words, an explicit attempt was made to link EIP to an existing model that already signified collaborative professional development in which the child was the focus and in where processes of experimentation and trial and error were acceptable, as long as they at least led to adult learning, if not improved outcomes for children.

After the first year of the RLC (September 2016 to June 2017), interviews were again held with the same 15 teachers in July 2017. This time, however, their purpose was to ascertain:

1. the post-intervention attitudes and behaviours of staff in relation to collaborative EIP (i.e. to determine participants' post-intervention OR type) and

2. any changes in relation to the benefits, costs and signifying factors associated with the ORP of collaborative EIP.

As before, interviews were recorded and transcribed. Data from the recordings were then analysed to determine the OR *type* of participants and their perspectives in relation to the three signifying of Benefit, Cost and Signification. Beginning with the post-intervention OR *type* of participants, as in the pre-intervention analysis, this was determined by looking at teachers' responses to questions 1 and 4 in Table 3.1. As can be seen in Figure 4.1, these responses suggest that post-intervention, while the existing Type 1 respondents remained in position, five respondents shifted from their original position to Type 1. Of these, one was the initial Type 4 rejecter (respondent #9); two moved upwards from Type 3 (respondents #8 and #12) and two moved across from Type 2 (respondents #2 and #6). Also interesting was that two further Type 2 respondents (#5 and #15), while remaining in their original quadrant, did demonstrate changes in their perceptions and behaviours that indicated they were moving closer to the Type 1 position. Examining the interview data of these respondents (and for the purposes of brevity ignoring for the most part the data of those who remained within their original quadrant), Figures 4.2 and 4.3 show the new hierarchy of codes that emerges as well as how these codes were situated according to rationality type. Exploring the data in detail illustrates a number of key shifts in perception related to the benefits, costs and signification associated with EIP.

Shifting from Type 3 (localised or non-collaborative research use): Beginning with those who moved from Types 3 to 1, it can be seen that key thematic codes for both of the individuals concerned included the realisation that collaborative EIP could have both local and wider *benefits*. In particular, this is highlighted by the thematic codes: *The ability to relate research to a real-life problem related to the Federation, Recognising benefits of collaborative research use* and *Recognising importance of wider research-informed collaboration*. Vignettes relating to these codes include:

**Figure 4.1. Allocation of Respondents According to Post-intervention OR Type.**

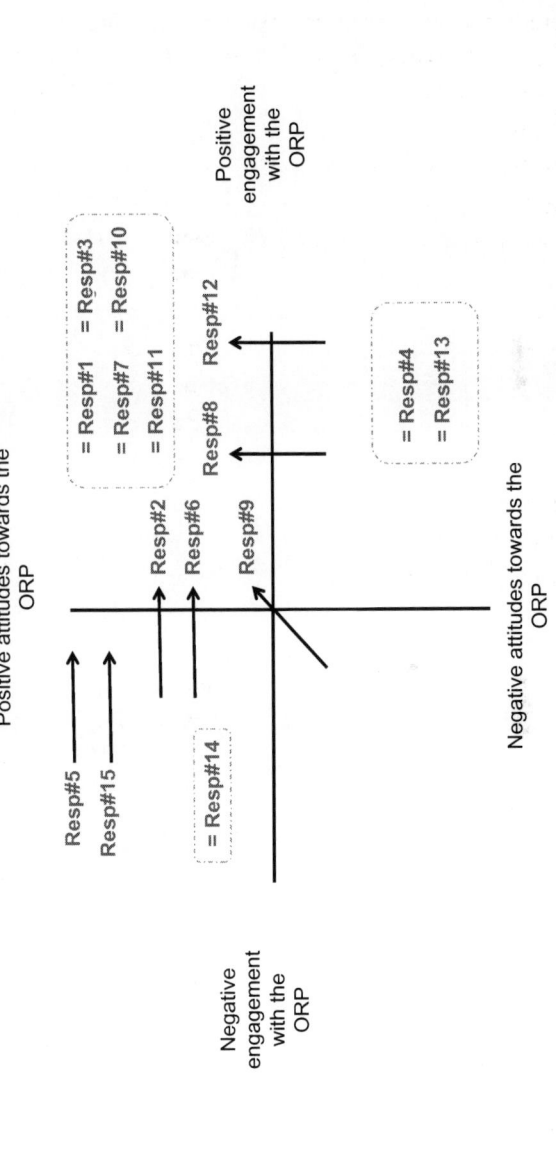

**Figure 4.2. The New Hierarchy of Thematic Codes.**

| Benefits | Cost | Signifying |
|---|---|---|
| Can relate research to a real-life problem | Time<br>• to engage (+)<br>• Competing priorities (+) | Useful collaborative endeavour which provides a route to better student outcomes |
| Recognising the benefits of collaborative research use | Access<br>• Being able to access (+) | Professionally exciting |
| Exploring and engaging | Overcoming perceived issues with engagement (+) | |
| Enables enquiry-related professional growth | Maintaining motivation | |
| Understanding how to engage | | |
| Can see impact | | |
| Sustaining the benefits | | |
| Extending the approach | | |
| Recognising the need to be systematic when using research | | |
| Collaborative orientation<br>• Recognising importance of common focus<br>• Recognising importance of wider research-informed collaboration | | |

**Figure 4.3. Allocation of Thematic Codes According to Respondent's New ORP Type.**

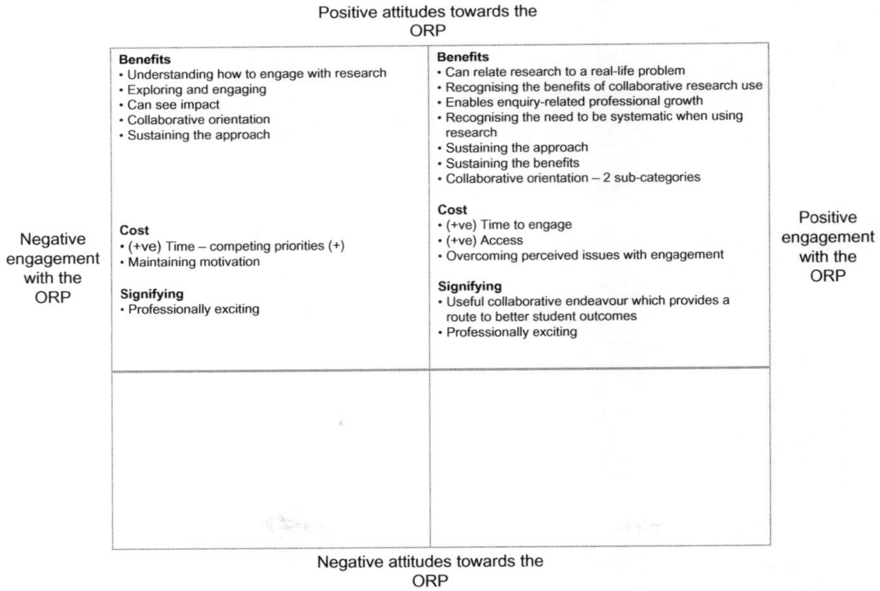

Positive attitudes towards the ORP

|  | Positive engagement with the ORP |
|---|---|
| **Negative engagement with the ORP** | **Benefits**<br>• Understanding how to engage with research<br>• Exploring and engaging<br>• Can see impact<br>• Collaborative orientation<br>• Sustaining the approach<br><br>**Cost**<br>• (+ve) Time – competing priorities (+)<br>• Maintaining motivation<br><br>**Signifying**<br>• Professionally exciting | **Benefits**<br>• Can relate research to a real-life problem<br>• Recognising the benefits of collaborative research use<br>• Enables enquiry-related professional growth<br>• Recognising the need to be systematic when using research<br>• Sustaining the approach<br>• Sustaining the benefits<br>• Collaborative orientation – 2 sub-categories<br><br>**Cost**<br>• (+ve) Time to engage<br>• (+ve) Access<br>• Overcoming perceived issues with engagement<br><br>**Signifying**<br>• Useful collaborative endeavour which provides a route to better student outcomes<br>• Professionally exciting |
|  |  |

Negative attitudes towards the ORP

*Engaging with research collaboratively has been powerful for lots of reasons – including in terms of attainment for our children. Obviously what we want to do is carry it on and see if the data continues to improve. In addition, conversations about learning across the federation have improved and that has had an impact on what we do as a school. I think people understand more now that they are doing these things not just because it's a fad. (Respondent #12)*

*[Working like this] everyone is involved and the conversations about research go across the federation and so it's given us the opportunity to share the research and to learn from projects that have gone on across the whole federation. (Respondent #8)*

At the same time, it was also noted by respondent #6 (an existing Type 1 teacher) that these two teachers who (unbeknown to respondent #6) had originally been identified as Type 3 had 'really enjoyed the collaborative activity… and I think they were surprised that they enjoyed it so much'.

Furthermore, respondents #8 and #12 could now also see that more localised, individual approaches were less effective. For example, one response coded as *Collaborative orientation – recognising importance of wider research-informed collaboration* observed that: '[having] time to talk motivates people and people share new ideas and you move forward very quickly. I think some people are doing their research in isolation and [that approach] is flawed' (respondent #8). Respondent #12 meanwhile noted that: 'I think because we have been working in cross-school groups, it was [more] powerful [then previous localised approaches]: the discussions were powerful and we knew what each other were doing. We knew what we were talking about, and it felt like a team, we knew what each other were doing. It felt like we were a team and it gave it much more momentum really.'

As the following quotes show, respondents were also keen to *sustain* and *extend* the *benefits* reaped during year one of the project:

> *This kind of research [activity] should never stop should it? It should lead onto something else and that's the beauty of it. It evolves and that's why it's quite exciting really. (Respondent #8)*

> *[Having gone through the process and seeing the difference it makes] what is happening now is that we are having conversations about how we want to keep this going. (Respondent #12)*

> *We'll keep it going, and seeing when you have a different cohort of children... it might be that we take our ideas [research-informed interventions] and use them with maths, so then they have a language of learning that [can be applied to a number of subjects]. (Respondent #8)*

Vitally both respondents also indicated that many of the perceived *costs* of engaging in collaborative EIP had now been ameliorated through the RLC approach: in particular, that *time to engage* in this way had been provided; that the design of the approach meant teachers were *able to access research*; and, crucially, that facilitated engagement with research was less daunting than previously expected (*overcoming perceived issues with engagement*). Example quotes for each of these cost codes are provided below:

*Time – to engage* (+)

> *Time to read through things was really helpful.*
> *(Respondent #12)*

> *[The approach] gave us structured support and it*
> *gave us a chance to talk a lot. It gave us the time to*
> *talk and share ideas and so I think that was really*
> *valuable. I don't think the research would have been*
> *as good, or as successful as it has been to date... if*
> *we'd not had that. (Respondent #8)*

*Access – being able to access* (+)

> *For me, I haven't read that kind of documentation*
> *in a long time. But actually I found it so useful*
> *because [in the past] that's the bit I've found hardest*
> *with the enquiry - having access [to research].*
> *(Respondent #12)*

> *You pointed us in the direction of sources [of*
> *research] and that was useful. (Respondent #8)*

*Engagement – overcoming perceived issues with*
*engagement* (+)

> *I [realise now that] it's not as daunting once you've*
> *done it, you know a couple of times. I had to read it*
> *twice, and I find I'm not in the practice of doing*
> *that, so I'd have to read it, scan it through and then*
> *go back and highlight it... in the end, I realised I*
> *could do it. (Respondent #12)*

A number of those who stayed as Type 3 teachers noted that they did not collaborate fully when developing EIPs, for example, 'I think it's difficult because [of the distance between schools] and the cover time to release us [to collaborate]' (respondent #4). This means there is further work moving forward to continue to develop the intervention in order to attempt to better support this group.

*Shifting from Type 2 (in agreement with the ORP but not yet engaging in it)*: In total, four Type 2 individuals shifted position: two moved towards Type 1 attitudes and behaviours and two became Type 1 individuals. Where individuals had moved but remained Type 2, it was clear that the approach had helped them *understanding how to engage* with research evidence. This is illustrated by the following quote:

> *I think when we initially started I was way out of my comfort zone to be honest, I'd never done anything like it before and it took a lot of getting my head around... I feel much more now that I do actually know where we're headed and the direction we need to go in. I mean, I'm still a bit – you know – fear and trepidation about going into next year, because [I worry about] 'am I getting this right?'. But the framework I in place and [its only when] you talk to other people you realise how far you have come on this journey. (Respondent #15)*

These respondents were also beginning to *explore and engage* with research and could *see impact* from what they were doing, but it was clear that they were yet to fully and systematically engage in EIP. As one noted: 'I think that's the problem with my approach [to engaging with the research]. [It hasn't been] sustainable this year – I've been dipping in and out'. And correspondingly that, 'I think there has to be one person who really continues to drive it... keeping it top of mind all the time' (respondent #5). In other words, it was felt by this respondent that further support was needed to help *maintain motivation* to continuously engage.

The one Type 2 teacher who remained in position noted that they had not meaningfully engaged with the research evidence as part of the process: 'What we did was more based on [our own teaching experience] and what we were seeing in our own rooms and with our own children rather than from looking at the wider research… the reading side slipped away really' (respondent #14). In part this lack of engagement was ascribed to a certain nervousness on the part of some Type 2 teachers to try something that might not succeed: 'they're nervous of the process' (respondent #7); 'moving forward we need to push colleagues to try something they genuinely don't know about' (respondent #2). Again these quotes serving to highlight that further work is required to continue to develop the intervention.

For those who did make it all the way to Type 1, it was also noted that this, in part, was because the RLC approach helped reduce *costs* such as *overcoming perceived issues with engagement*. As respondent #6 noted: 'I'm not one to sit and read through reams of research, because, probably time and everything else, but when we did the "everyone read a little bit" and then fed back on it, I found that much easier than I thought… because I didn't want to have to sit and read through tons of stuff'. It was also felt that the RLC approach helped highlight certain practices that ensured teachers got the most out of the process. For instance, as the following quotes highlight, it helped respondents recognise the need to be systematic when using research: '[I've really understood the need to] be tighter on what we are trialling and recording it effectively' (respondent #6); and 'going through the process] has shown us that we need to be clearer in our baseline (we haven't done that systematically enough in the past) so it's made us realise these things are really important so we can improve that' (respondent #2).

*Shifting from Type 4 (ORP rejecters)*: For the previous Type 4 rejecter — who had now moved to Type 1 — the biggest perceptional changes were related to the increased identification of the *benefits* and the mitigation of the *costs* of engaging in collaborative ORP. In particular, as a result of participating in the workshop activities and experiencing the workings of a learning community — as well as being reassured as to the intentions of the Federation's leaders — respondent #9's interview revealed a total transformation in terms of reported attitudes and behaviours. Here, the benefits of collaborative EIP were related to an enabling of their *enquiry-related professional growth*. Respondent #9 observed: 'I felt [the model] gave me permission to start looking deeper and start using research, looking at it which I loved' and, 'it shifted my thinking...It helped me think differently about how I look at the child, my current approach and what I might do to change that approach [in relation to the child]'. Previous issues of performativity were banished:

> *we have been brought up in a culture where you have to succeed... and that anything that comes down from on high, you have to try it and it has to work... [but with this approach] I felt assured that there was openness and honesty, and that we could actually say 'actually that was sheer utter crap. It didn't make any iota of difference, where can go now?'.*

And crucially these perceived benefits were reinforced through this respondent being able to *see impact*: '[as a result of this] all of my children have made progress, bar one... [and] I know that these children have become empowered in their learning which is what I want'.

Interestingly, these comments were very similar to those made by Type 1 respondents who remained as Type 1. For instance, respondent #11's statement relating to *enquiry-related professional growth* was that: '[important to maintaining my engagement] was the knowledge that it was OK to get it wrong. That didn't matter, because it's not necessarily finding the answer…it is a process and what I thought we would discover is not what we discovered which is interesting', thus, highlighting the similarity in perceptions in relation to the benefits associated with the freedom to experiment and to take warranted risks afforded by the RLC approach. With respondent #9 this perception of *benefits* was so powerful in fact that, moving forward, they were keen to *extend the approach* into other areas of their work. For example, they noted that: 'because the approach was useful it made me start thinking the thing that I would love is to take the whole process that we went through and apply it to other areas of education. I feel that this would both empower us [as teachers] and have an impact on teaching. And that's the bit because at the end of the day all we want is what's best for the children.' And that: 'last night we were talking about our curriculum and I thought "why don't we take the process we have just been through and the model and apply it to how we look at our curriculum"'.

For all those who shifted, their responses to the signifying elements of collaborative EIP could be characterised by two codes: collaborative EIP was a *useful collaborative endeavour which provides a route to better student outcomes*; and respondents found collaborative EIP *professionally exciting*. Example quotes here included the following:

> [Collaborative EIP signifies] The child at the centre, then the teacher drawing in information relevant to their school, then distilling it to children so that they could make a difference. (Respondent #12)

*I think if you can find something that's really getting your class going and making a real difference constantly and it's something that you can use in your everyday practice, then fantastic, really exciting. (Respondent #5)*

*It's about continuing how to look at ways in how children learn and are engaged in their learning and how you move that on: how you assess it and how you use that assessment to move their learning forwards. (Respondent #8)*

*[Collaborative EIP signifies] bringing about exciting change. (Respondent #9)*

To conclude, in this chapter, I have attempted to show that it is possible to develop an intervention based on initial analysis — using the ORS approach — and to then examine whether, as a result, people have shifted attitudinally and in terms of reported behaviour: with the ideal being to move people towards the ORP. As Figure 4.1 shows, the approach developed for the specific ORP of collaborative EIP appears to have been moderately successful, with five additional teachers indicating that they are now engaged in Type 1 behaviour and two more indicating that they are moving in this direction. This, I argue, has occurred because the intervention was specifically designed to tackle some of the key issues or *costs* that, pre-intervention, had been associated with collaborative EIP. At the same time, it had also sought to make clear the *benefits*, and attempted to ensure the *signification* associated with EIP could be linked to an existing and exciting model of teacher professionalism (i.e. the Finnish approach). Moving forward, however, a more scientific assessment of the efficacy of approaches, such as the one developed here, requires the testing of promising interventions via the use of randomised control trials or quasi-experimental approaches. Doing so will enable researchers to assess whether specific approaches do in fact change actual observed behaviours compared to a counter factual (e.g. a control group receiving no intervention, or in the case of a quasi-experimental approach a similar group to those treated).

In fact, an independent scientific evaluation of RLCs has been undertaken, albeit examining a slightly different version of the RLC approach to the one presented here (see Rose et al., 2017). To test this alternative version of the RLC model, I recruited 119 schools, with half then randomly allocated by Rose's team to an intervention group and half to a control group. With a team of colleagues I then worked with the intervention group, taking them through the RLC approach for two years. As Rose et al.'s (2017) evaluation shows, that version of the RLC approach did appear to increase instances of collaborative EIP at scale as well as a belief in the benefits of this type of approach. In other words, RLC-type approaches do appear to lead to more Type 1 behaviour. Moving forward therefore I suggest that social scientists can and should employ a qualitative ORS approach to provide clues as to how we can shift behaviour (and so what interventions might comprise). The testing of interventions meanwhile should then be undertaken using quantitative research which can reveal the extent to which interventions actually work to shift participants towards ORPs.

## NOTE

1. See: https://www.smithsonianmag.com/innovation/why-are-finlands-schools-successful-49859555/

# CHAPTER 5

# ATTENDING TO THE SIGNIFIER – USING 'SCENES' TO MAKE OPTIMAL RATIONAL POSITIONS MORE ATTRACTIVE

As the last two chapters have shown, to move people to the 'Type 1' ORP set out in Figure 1.2, we have three potential points of action open to us. First we can attend to the costs people associate with a specific ORP and try and reduce the barriers to people's engagement and/or their perceptions of these barriers. Second we can do more to highlight the benefits of the ORP, in particular by better linking the benefits for the long-term collective to those for the short-term self. Finally we can attend to the signification or meaning associated with the ORP and so attempt to improve the attractiveness of any given ORP's brand.

Yet while these three potential areas of focus exist, most approaches to support engagement with ORPs seem to attend solely to the costs and benefits associated with such positions. For example, at my local leisure centre there is a poster in the changing room extolling the benefits of swimming for 30 minutes three times a week. As well as listing these benefits, the poster also provides various prices for using the swimming pool at different times and according to different categories of customer. The main imagery on the poster, however, is simply a photograph of someone swimming – there is no attractive signification to encourage individuals to make the decision to swim. Likewise is England's 'Drink Aware' campaign, designed to encourage adults to drink less alcohol.[1] Fundamentally the campaign is fact-driven: it provides information on recommended units of alcohol per week; it illustrates what a unit of alcohol comprises (e.g. in terms of the number of pints of beer or gin and tonics it represents); it also provides advice in terms of how one might lower one's drinking and tools to help measure it. As with the swimming campaign, however, all we are shown graphically are photographs both of people drinking and of them not drinking. One final example is the website for 'Climate Care',[2] which is similarly perfunctory. Advice and tips for reducing carbon emissions are provided here. There is little, however, in the way of imagery. While only a small selection, what these examples show is that the signification aspect of ORPs tends to be consigned to the background; with the hope being that the Kantian *should* type nature of these ORPs will be enough to convince people to engage with/in the activities in question. In other words, the logic of such approaches is something along the lines of: swimming is beneficial, swimming is cheap, you want to live a long healthy life so therefore you should swim.

In Chapter 2, however, I suggested that ORPs exist within the more general gamut of consumerism and consumption. This is because ORPs require us to make choices about how we commit finite resources such as money and time. I also showed, using the example of Nespresso and Bialetti coffee makers and my thought process as I chose between them, how other consumer brands operate to help steer our decision-making by making specific choices more attractive. Brands are able to steer our behaviour like this because we latch on to their signifying aspect as a means to reaffirm specific aspects about who we perceive ourselves to be, as well as send messages about who we are to others. In other words, brands can operate in this way because consumption is more than something we engage in to fulfil needs – rather it is an activity that enables us to position ourselves within a wider web of signification (Baudrillard, 1968). Because of this consumer brands rarely, if ever, simply rely just on promoting cost and benefit alone.

In fact, the most successful brands are those that create worlds that invite us in and excite or enthuse us such that we want to be continually associated with them. With these brands, not only do we purchase but we also develop brand loyalty. One only has to visit any shopping centre anywhere in the country to see how companies such as Hollister seek to inspire their customers. Sticking with this example, as well as their unconventional beach hut style shop fronts, with dark pumping interiors, Hollister deliberately plays on 'the *fantasy* of Southern California. Inspired by beautiful beaches, open blue skies, and sunshine, Hollister lives the dream of an endless summer'.[3] Hollister as a brand thus entices you into a different world and offers you the taste of exciting difference. You want to shop there and keep coming back to stay part of the Hollister experience. A key question therefore is how we might replicate this attractiveness and loyalty for ORPs? The answer I suggest lies in the semiotic concept of 'scenes'.

As suggested elsewhere (e.g. Brown, 2016) scenes can be thought of as representing situations in which people are doing something noticeably different from the 'norm'. By norm I mean the average day-to-day experiences one generally encounters; for instance, the conversations we usually have, the genres of music we generally find ourselves listening to, the variety or type of restaurants available for us to eat in (and so on). The idea of 'situation', meanwhile, can and should be interpreted broadly. For instance, a situation could occur entirely in one place, but it could also represent activity undertaken by many people in many places. Importantly, however, no matter what the situation, the break from the norm offered up by the scene will be something that signifies vibrant and exciting new perspectives, i.e. new ways of thinking or behaving. Taking just two examples of scenes: London's 1970s punk-rock music scene can be seen as representing a revolt by alienated youths in a post-industrial Britain in economic decline. Punk became a major cultural phenomenon that not only spawned a new type of music but also redefined how people could look (in terms of fashion and adornments as well as general appearance) as part of a process of expressing disaffection. In terms of art, Malevich's suprematism movement was born of the idea that all art is just an imitation of nature and for it to be original it must eschew any form of replication. The result of this pursuit for originality was Malevich's groundbreaking painting of a black square on canvas (*Black Square*, 1915). Designed to privilege the invoking of emotion over visual phenomenon, Malevich's work went on to inspire *constructivism* and is considered to be the *point zero* of modern art more generally. Scenes therefore serve to enrich our lives by (for instance) opening up exciting new genres to explore, perspectives through which we can understand and activities for us engage in.

As a concept, scenes may be thought of as sharing a number of specific characteristics (Brown, 2016):

- They are recognisable – scenes will often signify a distinct genre, style or a new school of thought and so their outputs can be easily attributed to the scene in question (e.g. this is how we can recognise constructivist art; this is an example of punk). Likewise scenes may represent specific actions: here, as well as the acts themselves, there is also likely to be scenic affordances in terms of, say, physical appearance, dress code and ways of talking or discourse that serve to set members of the scene apart (e.g. this is how we recognise skate boarders or surfers).

- An important aspect of any scene is its attractiveness and I explore this in more detail below using the notion of 'scenic capital'. Nonetheless, it goes without saying that scenes and the difference they offer will only flourish if people find their signification appealing, exciting and vibrant.

- It is possible to both start and join scenes. Whether we join a scene will be determined by a number of things, including the attractiveness of a scene to us, but also, importantly, whether we possess the requisite skills to do so and often even the geography of where the scene is situated.

- Scenes that are truly vibrant and enduring will survive the coming and going of individuals. As a result, scenes are best viewed as being organic, materialising via a 'natural' (rather than an imposed) emergence of people, ideas and activities.

Although this outline of what scenes are perhaps sounds a tad grandiose, scenes do not have to be. When researching the notion of scenes some of the people I spoke to included the owners of one of my favourite coffee shops – The Haberdashery in Crouch End. The owners of The Haberdashery told me how, in conceptualising their shop, they had tried to recreate in North London the type of atmosphere they experienced in relation to the (*fika*) coffee scene in Gothenburg. Here then an initial attempt at difference was established by the owners but it was subsequently taken up and perpetuated by the customers and staff who embraced *fika*. Scenes can thus be either grand or small scale (they can represent both punk music and a simple shop), but what they do have to be is identifiable: you immediately know when you encounter or arrive at one.

Scenes are relevant to the analysis of ORPs because the process of signalling through more general consumption (including that of ORPs) also applies to scenes. In other words, in a world where we are able to consume pretty much anything we desire (from concrete 'things' to less tangible constructs such as lifestyles, experiences and environments), then scenes, like ORPs, should also be considered within a broader understanding of what comprises a 'consumer object'. This means therefore that the signification that is associated with scenes is ultimately something that, if desirable, can be appropriated by consumers (for instance, via direct purchase or through engagement, action and association). Furthermore in a system of consumption where we are continually signalling to one another, there is a tendency amongst individuals to embrace anything that helps them signify desirable new difference. As a result, there is a continuous development of consumer 'objects' that offer something cutting edge – a type of signification not experienced before. This implies therefore that there is also a demand for new scenes that can enable us to engage with and relate to novel ideas and lifestyles (and through our consumption of them) signify that we are now associated with the scene in question.

Clearly, however, this difference has to be attractive – something we may think of as a scene's 'capital'. Given the personal nature of signification, scenic capital will, first of all, be a function of what the scene means to us as individuals – a scene's distinctiveness might tap into, for instance, a facet of the self we wish to express; or perhaps encountering the scene invokes a desire in relation to how we wish to live. But scenic capital will also be connected to whether we believe our association with the scene might affect our relationships with others and the attractiveness of these new or changed relationships. For instance, how being part of the scene serves to position us in relation to (for example) those inside the scene already, our current friends or peers, those outside the scene and so on. To return to punk music as an example, we may get into punk for a number of reasons, but these are likely to reflect both internal meanings and how we express our internal selves to others. For instance, the harshness of the new sound may energise us but if we know others know we are listening to it, then it represents a way to express our disaffection. The vibrancy of the fashion may appeal, but it will also allow us to reposition ourselves as anti-establishment. Returning to the earlier analysis above, scenic capital therefore relates to our beliefs in terms of what is being signified and how this new signification sits within the broader web of signs through which we already make meaning (or possibly how it has disrupted this web and how 'meaning' changes as a result).

To really take off however, a scene has to be attractive to many people. For example, the scene might represent a new must visit location – a place (much like Machu Picchu) whose passport stamps represent new badges of honour. For more temporal scenes, such as music or art, where the aim typically is to disrupt the status quo in order that new points of view can be incorporated, the attractiveness of this disruption will be a function of how wedded to the old ways potential audiences are. Often the perspectives offered by temporal scenes can also be presented in terms of choices: right or wrong, old or new, austerity or bankruptcy, them or us. For scenes that seek to require us to make such a choice, scenic capital is accrued by those scenes that are best able to 'market' themselves to potential audiences, leading them to want to be associated with one side or another. Of course, the aim or purpose of this type of marketing will depend on the activity in question. In terms of politics, for instance, the aim is likely to involve dominance. For example echo chambers, in seeking to develop policies that appeal to the electorate, will be attempting to form a kind of discursive hegemony; in other words, to convince as many voters as possible that their proposed way forward is the most appropriate, while seeking to ensure that those who oppose such perspectives seem 'old fashioned' or even 'backwards looking' (Lister, 2000).

Returning to education, in Brown (2016) I present the case of the London Borough of Tower Hamlets as an example of a scene. In 1997 Tower Hamlets was the worst performing local education authority in England (149th out of 149 in terms of its performance). In an amazing transformation, however, over a space of less than 10 years, Tower Hamlets has moved from a position of poor performance, to one in which it was being praised for its high-quality services, sustained improvement in education outcomes, excellent partnership work and being highly ambitious for its children and young people. Analysing how and why Tower Hamlets dramatically improved its performance reveals a number of vital scenic attributes. These include the exciting and visionary discourse of new leaders who were committed to educational excellence; a distinctive approach to school improvement grounded in an understanding of local context and needs and the emergence of a different and enduring culture based on shared values, purpose and endeavour. Together these attributes led to Tower Hamlets being viewed as an attractive educational environment which enabled it to attract better teachers and school leaders which in turn served to further reinforce the culture and unique approach being pursued by the borough.

More generally, it is possible to argue that the analysis of Tower Hamlets highlights two key aspects of scenes that may be useful to thinking about how they can be employed in the pursuit of maximising well-being: (1) that scenes such as Tower Hamlets possess distinctive discourses and sets of behaviours that in turn helps them develop a long-lasting and appealing culture. These can be discourses/behaviours that are initiated and/or propagated in 'top-down' ways (i.e. through the use of leaders) as was the case in Tower Hamlets or, equally, discourses and behaviours can grow organically as a congruence of like-minded people come together. Here the importance of relationships and social networks comes to the fore since individuals with high social capital are likely to be best placed to attract others to the scene. The culture that results is often likely to represent what we might consider to be a new *genre*: for instance, the spawning of hip hop in 1970's New York or the recent *slow food* movement in Italy. But, as in Tower Hamlets, such a culture can also easily be centred on more welfare maximising behaviours such as school improvement. Furthermore and importantly and (2) this discourse/behaviours is catalytic in nature. In other words it serves to act as a change agent that moves a group of people from displaying one distinct set of discourses and behaviours to another.

Bringing this analysis together, it is my argument therefore that the signifying aspect of ORPs has so far been neglected. This means that ORPs fundamentally rely on cost and benefit type approaches to encourage people to engage with (i.e. consume) them. Since ORPs are types of consumer goods more attention should be given to what is – or what could potentially be – signified by any given ORP. If practical examples of people engaging with the ORP occurs in such a way that they signify attractive difference it may be possible that specific enactments of ORPs could emerge as the creation of scenes. As I show in Brown (2016), as well as punk and modern abstract art, scenes can represent activity that is in the same welfare maximising ball park to that likely to be required by ORPs. It would seem feasible therefore that considering any of the examples of ORPs set out in the introduction, that new movements could be seeded that approach (for example) reducing carbon emissions, healthy eating, regular exercise, reducing drinking, etc., in exciting new ways that might make others want to become part of these new movements/ORP scenes. Taking the examples at the beginning of this chapter for instance, a 'drink aware' related scene could, for example, see (only) non-alcoholic drinks served in exciting and hip new venues designed to make abstinence feel cool as well as work to make us healthier; perhaps drawing on the gin scene that already exists, alcohol-free substitute spirits such as Seedlip[4] could be used as the basis of new 1920's style speakeasies in which the illicit nature of the drink is that it is non-alcoholic.

As social scientists, however, we need to draw on our research skills to help facilitate these scenes. As I illustrate in Chapters 3 and 4 it is possible to develop interventions that help people behave in ways that maximise welfare by exploring and then responding to their views and perspectives in relation to the ORP in question. The specific intervention I discuss, however, ultimately had a semi-imposed nature to it, in the sense that it was led and mandated by the school leadership of the Chestnut Learning Federation. With scenes, the attractiveness of what is on offer and the people involved in it has to be compelling enough to make people want to engage voluntarily. As such, once we as social scientists understand why people don't engage with ORPs, we will need to work with other stakeholders to transform this understanding into exciting propositions and movements that reverse this position. Likewise, when we uncover instances or case studies of individuals engaging in ORPs in potentially exciting new ways we need to document these. In both cases these positions then need to be publicised and marketed – to become a fundamental part of the ORP's brand so that others get to hear about these new vibrant, exciting and attractive approaches to engaging in ORPs and want to join such scenes or establish their own. In some cases the original scene may be directly joined or replicated. In other cases this may not be possible, but people still affiliate themselves with the scene in question. What is most important in order to achieve change, however, is that individuals associate the attractiveness of the scene with engaging in the ORP and so begin to increasingly 'consume' (and in according with the ORP) in order to signify their association. When this happens people will begin to act in ways that serves to maximise overall welfare.

## NOTES

1. See: https://www.drinkaware.co.uk

2. See: https://climatecare.org/50-ideas-for-shrinking-your-carbon-footprint/

3. See: https://www.facebook.com/hollister/info?tab=page_info.

4. See: seedlipdrinks.com

# CHAPTER 6

# LESSONS FOR SOCIAL SCIENCE MOVING FORWARD

It seems logical, as a consumer society unwilling to change its economic model, that we should seek to tackle many of the problems we currently face through the adoption of a consumerist perspective. As such, since ORPs involve consumption and the reallocation of finite resource (money, time, energy, etc.), we can and should apply to them the rules that govern other forms of consumer behaviour. As I note in Chapter 2, the work of Baudrillard (1968) shows how consumption is driven by perceptions of the benefits and costs of consuming as well as the idea of signification: the imagery invoked and transmitted through the act of consumption. I also illustrate in Chapter 4 that it is seemingly possible to develop interventions that address these three factors in realms not typically associated with consumerism (in this case the use of research evidence by teachers and school leaders). Furthermore, in Chapter 5 I show how in some instances signification can be so compelling that behaving in new ways can be almost irresistible. Correspondingly, while the main task of the social sciences has traditionally been to explain social phenomena (Elster, 2007), this new perspective means that social scientists can also be the instigators of change.

A key challenge of course is getting individuals to change their long-term behaviour. In their seminal psychological study, Kegan and Lahey (2009) note that, of the people told by their doctor that they must change their behaviour or risk putting their lives in jeopardy, only one in seven do actually change. Likewise, Kegan and Lahey suggest that, on average, people who diet typically regain 107% of what they lost. Any attempt to change people's behaviours thus requires individuals to make both *technical* and *adaptive* changes. Here technical change relates to people's understanding of what they need to do, whereas adaptive change corresponds to how secure their commitment to doing something different actually is. In other words adaptive change involves altering values and assumptions in addition to behavioural change. As a consequence, if how people view the world, their image of themselves and their beliefs shift positively, this helps them to also change how they act. In the examples provided by Kegan and Lahey, even though individuals knew informationally what they had to do there was no adaptive change, i.e. there was no fundamental shift in beliefs regarding their behaviour. As a result, people's actions remained as they were or eventually reverted back to their previous state.

With the issue of climate change the opposite currently seems to hold true. Up to now, the emphasis from the scientific community would appear to be focused on highlighting the need for change. For example, in 2013 the Consensus Project[1] was launched by researchers. The aim of the project was to show that the scientific community was united in its belief that climate change was happening and needed to be halted. Furthermore, as Warren Pearce argues in *The Guardian*, this notion of consensus subsequently became part of former US President Barack Obama's election campaign messaging.[2] The focus on consensus is grounded in the notion that the public's perception of scientific concord is a *gateway* belief: that once the public understand that scientists uniformly believe that climate change is happening, they too will believe that it is happening and so will support the need for change (evidence for this notion of gateway beliefs is provided in van der Linden, Leiserowitz, Feinberg, & Maibach, 2015). Pearce rightly points out, however, that now that the majority of the public do believe in climate change it is time to move the conversation on. This is because while belief exists, as noted earlier, action is yet to take root (Leiserowitz et al., 2017). In other words, beliefs and values regarding climate change have shifted so that climate change is seen by the public as a concern, but what people are unsure of is how they can make a concrete positive difference (i.e. know what technical changes are required) and what concrete impact their steps might have. Pearce and colleagues (2017) also suggest that little has been done to foster change by individuals.

As the analysis in Chapter 4 begins to outline, both technical and adaptive changes can be achieved if we engage in semiotic analysis and then take action based on this analysis. This is because, as I illustrate in Figure 1.2, individuals can be divided into four types according to their attitudes towards and engagement in any given ORP. Furthermore we can use Baudrillard's work to guide our semiotic exploration in order to examine for each behavioural type: (1) the *meaning* that is *signified*/we can signify by taking a decision; (2) the *costs* or how difficult it will be to undertake the action required and (3) the *usefulness* or the *benefits* that result from taking the decision (see Figure 2.1). Correspondingly, we can examine the differences in perceptions and actions between those individuals that do believe and do engage in acts that accord to the ORP and those that don't. Once we have explored beliefs and behaviours in this way we can then, as I show in Chapter 4, start to develop interventions grounded in our understanding of these differences. Here, interventions (or suites of interventions) should be designed with the explicit purpose of closing the gaps between those in the Type 1 quadrant and others. As such, based on what emerges from the semiotic analysis, they must have explicit aims, such as lowering the costs of engagement with the ORP or changing people's perceptions of these costs; promoting the benefits to individuals of engaging in the ORP; and/or helping people experience these benefits first hand. Finally, these interventions should also attempt to make engaging with the ORP so compelling and attractive, an option that people willingly want to behave differently. This latter aspect can and should also recognise that signification flows through relationships, not only between concepts but also between people. As such if the people we are connected to are involved in activities while are also opinion formers (i.e. possess significant social capital), they are likely to influence us and others to also engage in such activities (see Berger, 2016, for a more detailed analysis of social influence; although it is also clear that not everyone is influenced by everybody).

Suggestions for the nature of the interventions that might help us do this already exist. For instance, the following have all been previously posited as a means to help people behave more rationally: (1) improving social prestige or recognition (Olson, 1965); (2) developing a cooperative social value orientation as well as group identity and solidarity (Dawes, van de kragta, & Orbell, 1988; Rose & Colman, 2007); (3) framing the ORP so that it better signifies the benefits to the group in question (Rose & Colman, 2007); (4) showing people what to do or make it clear how other people are behaving to achieve the ORP (Bacharach, 1999, 2006) and (5) making it clear that personal efficacy is high, i.e. that individuals can achieve wider change through individual behaviour

(Kerr, 1992) (although it should be noted that none of these factors really deals with signification). But at the same time interventions need to be grounded in the very specific nature of the context in which the semiotic analysis was undertaken. In particular, it is clear that what might comprise a scene for some people may not be appealing for others. This is where the efforts of social scientists must come to the fore. We must use our analytical skills to understand whether we simply need to help individuals see the world in the same way as Type 1 individuals see it. For instance, do Type 1 individuals simply have a better understanding of costs and benefits than others? Or do we need to work with stakeholders to help them develop very specific interventions grounded in the evidence we have gathered about these groups?

What's more, to help create new scenes social scientists need to spend significant time examining the wider web of signification that relates to the attractiveness or not of the ORP. With a scene, attractiveness comes from how the signification associated with the scene taps into facets of the self (our personal brand) or offers disjunctures from previous ways of being. To understand the attractiveness of an ORP thus requires in-depth exploration of the kinds of adjectives and imagery currently associated with the concept and finding out whether what is currently attractive to some groups (such as Type 1 and 2 individuals) could be attractive to others. Or, alternatively, whether a new signification needs to be seeded, based on new conceptualisations of what the ORP is and means. Correspondingly, developing this understanding may require multiple iterative rounds of research as webs of signification are traced and new ideas introduced and responses to them ascertained. For example, returning to the Chestnut Learning Federation, interview data suggested the notion of evidence-informed professional development was linked by some Type 1 individuals to the Finnish model of teaching and learning, which they found inherently exciting due to its connotations of professionalisation and the international recognition of Finland's educational success. Recognising that the Finnish model might prove attractive to other groups, its key facets were summarised and presented to those who were rejecters of EIP. This group too found it exciting and attractive, as did Type 2 and 3 individuals.

Because the Finnish model proved generally compelling, key aspects of the approach developed for Chestnut were explicitly linked to it throughout the year-long process. Using the characteristics of the Finnish model has been instrumental in helping rejecters reevaluate what evidence-use means. Once EIP began to be linked to the idea of collaborative professional development in which the child was the focus and in where processes of experimentation and trial and error were acceptable, as long as they led to adult learning, the understanding of the potential benefits of the new way of working began to increase and perceived costs fell. In addition, as the data in Chapter 4 show, this approach helped Type 3 and 4 individuals to start thinking about what participation in collaborative evidence-informed discussion meant, what it implied for them as professionals and what it signified to their colleagues outside of the Federation. While I do not have the data to suggest that the Chestnut approach was viewed from the outside as a scene, for those inside the Federation, because of the re-signification that was seeded through associations with teaching and learning in Finland, engaging in the act of EIP started to become associated with professionalism and professional autonomy. As such it represented something that teachers within the Federation actively wanted to be associated with.

What this suggests is that, while starting brand new scenes may be too tricky without the help of skilled marketers, we are situated in a world of concepts that are linked together through signifying webs. Moving forward therefore, to help find ways of encouraging individuals to consume ORPs, social scientists need to consciously map out these webs and find attractive associations that can be used as hooks to encourage adaptive change. This perhaps seems relatively more difficult than understanding how to reduce costs or increase benefits. But in fact it simply relies on us remembering the basics of empiricism. We are all consumers and are at all times surrounded by signs that we interpret. If we find concepts appealing, then others are likely to as well, and assuming we are from similar contexts and backgrounds to those we research, we are likely to exist within the same signifying webs as they do. Correspondingly we should note how we feel when we find ourselves surrounded by Danes cycling across Copenhagen, come across a buzzing new coffee shop or find an album that forms the soundtrack of our summer. Likewise we need to remember the coolness that exudes from watching people surf, skate or BMX, or the inspiration we gain when we pick up on novel ideas such as Paul McCartney's 'Meat Free Mondays' or the slow food or travel movements, or find ourselves amongst a new community or group of practitioners that has found an exciting alternative way to live or work. We should also consider how these ideas might relate or could be transferred to other facets of our lives. This is because it is by developing this encyclopaedia of potential scenic ideas and working out how they do or could make other people feel and behave that we can help understand how to improve an ORP's brand or the process though which it might be consumed. And if we can use our research to help shift patterns of consumption so that people engage in more optimal and rational behaviour because we have helped make doing so more attractive, then, as researchers, we will have truly achieved impact.

## NOTES

1. See: http://theconsensusproject.com

2. See: https://www.theguardian.com/science/political-science/2017/aug/01/well-never-tackle-climate-change-if-academics-keep-the-focus-on-consensus?CMP=Share_iOSApp_Other

# APPENDIX: FULL ANALYSIS OF THE INTERVIEW DATA FROM CHAPTER 3

In Chapter 3 I provided an abridged version of the interview analysis. Here, the findings for each quadrant are now explored in full, with findings organised, first by benefit, cost and signifying (BCS) value, and then by their mid-level and initial codes, thus providing a comprehensive description of the perspectives of respondents in relation to their ORP perspectives. The analysis begins by exploring views of these in the Type 1 quadrant.

*Type 1*: Beginning with the benefits that were signified by EIP, five mid-level and nine initial codes were identified within the Type 1 quadrant. The first of these mid-level codes was *recognises the benefits of using research*, which highlights respondents' beliefs that the regular use of research to inform practice would result in better outcomes for children. For instance, respondents noted that the focus of EIP needed to be about improving children's outcomes '[when you know] things could be better or more effective' (respondent #3). Participants in this quadrant could also readily identify leadership support directed at encouraging EIP (mid-level

code: *recognises school/federation level of support for EIP*).
For example that senior leaders with the federation were
scheduling the school timetable to allow collaboration: '[name
of senior leader] makes it work because he timetables meet-
ings [so that we can all attend]' (respondent #11).

Responses within the Type 1 quadrant also highlighted the
*enquiry mindset* of participants, which was demonstrated in
three specific ways. First was a *reflection on academic
research* by respondents; this code often reflected the
responses of those who had relatively recently completed an
undergraduate degree, Master's degree or even PhD, typically
alongside their teaching role. As a result of being in a situation which required them to actively combine study with
work, these respondents had developed a mindset of continuously reflecting on how the research they were engaging with
might support their teaching practice: 'I do try to use that
[the research] to inform practice at all times. I often find in
my head I'm thinking "How does this impact the children, or
my own learning?"' (respondent #1); 'I start thinking about
how I could develop that with the children' (respondent #10).

The *enquiry mindset* of participants was also highlighted
by responses which showed they *felt able to experiment and*
that they knew *how to experiment*, thus maximising the *benefits* they might get from research. Beginning with the first of
these, it was apparent that participants understood the utility
of experimentation and accepted the risks involved in doing
so. For instance, one noted: 'it can be difficult sometimes, but
I think you've got to be open to trying something new.
So ... if you read something and you think "Oh I wouldn't
mind having a go" it could go completely wrong. And
its having the *confidence* to accept that' (respondent #1).
Knowing *how to experiment* effectively was also a key fea-
ture of the responses of this group. For example respondents
understood the need to try to iteratively refine approaches to

maximise their effectiveness. As one noted: 'how often do we need to do [interventions] and how smartly can we do them so they have the most impact?' (respondent #7).

Participants more generally discussed the importance of having a *collaborative orientation* as a way of informing practice. For example one respondent noted the importance of *learning conversations* as a way of assessing whether and how new practices should be adopted, noting that as part of these there are a number of key considerations: 'if we are discussing something we may want to introduce, we often then say "well what's the purpose?" ... "How will this impact? How will we know?"' (respondent #1). One perceived benefit of engaging in learning conversations was that they challenged complacency and the formation of poor habits (i.e. doing things simply because they had 'always been done that way'; respondent #3). Learning conversations also enabled participants to engage in new ideas; '[otherwise] there is the danger that you don't remain current and abreast of everything' (respondent #10). Learning conversations were universally seen as being strengthened by research — again leading to an increased perception of the *benefits* of research.

*Networked learning conversations* that involved participants from across all three schools were also viewed as positive (as well as reflecting participants' *network orientation:* Daly, 2010). As one respondent noted: 'so an organization like this, part of the strength is that we can learn from each other, we know its powerful when we do it' (respondent #7). Practice and research sharing formed a prominent aspect of these conversations and participants also displayed a *network orientation* in that they *knew who to turn to for support,* i.e. that they were able to identify who within the federation might support them with engaging in EIP if required. Also that respondents *knew where to go to access research,* i.e. they could identify who and where they might go to access research.

Moving to the *cost* value, two mid-level codes were identified, both of which are related to the costs of EIP. The first of these was *time*, which was often regarded as a barrier to achieving even more (with the initial level coding reflecting the need to find *time to do it right*). Included here was the time needed to ensure sufficient good quality research could be drawn on: 'it takes time to find it' (respondent #11). *Sharing with colleagues* or the brokerage of research or research-informed strategies was also seen as key but time consuming, since it was recognised that sharing is only effective when research is 'effectively translated' (respondent #11) ('you've got to know how to translate it'; respondent #10).

Finally, in terms of the *signifying* values of EIP, respondents suggested that, to them, EIP signalled the presence of *reflective, empowered teachers who constantly improve their practice*. At the same time, findings here also suggest that respondents viewed the use of research as something that would provide the *confidence to collaborate* with others across the federation: the use of research thus seen as providing a firm basis upon which to debate and engage in discussion around effective forms of teaching and learning. For instance, responses to the question 'when I say research informed teaching, what image does that convey to you?' included: 'empowering, confidence and exciting' (respondent #1); 'knowledge, relevancy and informing' (respondent #10); 'an evidence-informed teacher is someone that has the confidence to open themselves up to being challenged' (respondent #1); 'a reflective teacher. A teacher that's really challenged themselves to improve' (respondent #11); 'its having the confidence to change things, and to look at things and to take that [research] onboard and to change the way you are working' (respondent #3).

*Type 2*: Moving now to the Type 2 quadrant and beginning again with the *benefits*, four mid-level and initial codes were identified. The first of these was *recognises school/federation level of support for EIP*. Here responses suggested, for example, that: 'over the last year it's been more highlighted [as something we should do] … and the language of using research-based evidence to inform your practice … it's become more of our vocabulary' (respondent #14); likewise: 'it's a culture that's become sort of recognised as "this is the way that we should be working all the time", that we can work like this … we can be creative about things' (respondent #15). Responses also indicated an *enquiry mindset* since participants also *felt able to experiment*: 'it's very trial and error … but yes I feel I've got that freedom to experiment a little bit' (respondent #5). This type of mindset thus likely to make teachers more open to using research as part of a process of experimentation.

As with the Type 1 quadrant, *learning conversations* (reflecting participant's *collaborative orientation*) were often used and seen as a beneficial way of challenging entrenched practice that might not always be effective: 'they stop us doing things … because you've always done it' (respondent #2); '[we ask] if it's not working then why isn't it working? [Is] there another way of doing things?' (respondent #14). As before, learning conversations were seen as being strengthened by research but, for these participants, this was less well established: 'we've talked about [research] a little bit, like five minutes at a speed dating style staff meeting … they're becoming more knowing that [practice] has to be backed up by [research]' (respondent #2).

Respondents in this quadrant also actively connected with colleagues in other schools in order to collaborate and learn from each other through *networked learning conversations* (again reflecting their *network orientation*). While this collaboration involved sharing it also involved the hallmarks of effective brokerage (e.g. Rogers, 2003), where underpinning principles were discussed with questions asked such as 'how did you do that?' or 'what [exactly] did you use that for?' (respondent #5), there was also practical application: 'we've tried lots of ways of doing things' (respondent #15). Moving forward it was also hoped that this collaboration would increase and also extend to EIP.

Four mid-level codes were identified for *cost*, of these, three were related to the time costs associated with engaging in EIP. For this quadrant, such costs were associated with the *time [needed] to do it right*, i.e. engaging with research effectively and meaningfully. More specifically, this time cost included: 'time to find out about the research, time to find out how to implement it and the time that it's going to take to do it differently when you're very busy ... [for a new research-informed approach or piece of evidence] it's going to take me time to read up on it, it's going to take me time to translate that into practical classroom activities and it's going to take me time to do it differently for a while until it becomes an integral part of my practice' (respondent #2).

What's more the cost of time also stretched to *sharing with colleagues*: ensuring that colleagues, such as teaching assistants (TA), understood how to use the approach as well. In both cases there was an anxiety about finding this time (*making time*), but it was felt that such issues would be manageable if protected time was allocated: '[ideally someone would say] this is your research time, go and do that. Don't think about planning. Don't think about class. You've got an afternoon to solely focus on your research' (respondent #6). One final cost value code was the cost of *access*. Here some expressed a worry as to whether they might understand formal academic research: 'I guess sometimes, thinking back to research and papers, it's the jargon that's used [sometimes you] read and think "what was that about?"' (respondent #14).

In terms of the *signifying* values, it was clear that respondents in this quadrant associated EIP with the qualities of the *enquiry mindset* expressed by those already engaged in research-use (i.e. those in quadrants Type 1 and Type 3) with that mindset then *providing a route to better practice*. More specifically, EIP was associated with teachers who reflect using research and develop deeper pedagogic knowledge as a result; who are willing to try new approaches; and who experiment to take risks to improve practice. What's more research-use was also seen to providing *confidence to collaborate* and a secure basis for evidence-informed teachers to be both collaborative and network orientated. This is nicely expressed in the following quote: '[a evidence informed teacher is] somebody who is confident in what they are doing, confident in their job, knows best practice, willing to try new things' (respondent #6).

*Type 3*: Within the Type 3 quadrant there were five *benefit* codes, one *cost* code and one *signifying* code. In contrast to the first two quadrants, however, two of the *benefit* codes indicated negative perspectives and a further use code represented a localised focus. The first of the positive codes was *recognises the benefits of using research*. In other words, it was thought by respondents in this quadrant that using research could result in better practice. This is nicely reflected in the response of following interviewee who stated that: 'I need [to use research] to address problems in my classroom, to inform me about what I'm going to do and to gain' (respondent #4). Others noted that because they had just taught a difficult cohort of children, they had turned to research to provide them with specific pedagogic strategies. Overall, however, the responses of those allocated to this

quadrant tended to reflect a more reactive rather than continuous engagement with research: 'it [engagement with
research] is mainly a reaction to things that are happening in
the classroom, not something that's been ongoing' (respondent #13).

It was also apparent that respondents within this quadrant
exhibited an *enquiry mindset*. This was indicated first by participants' *reflection on academic research*. Here, as before, this
code often applied to the responses of those who had relatively
recently completed a degree, or post-graduate qualification: 'I
think partly because I have studied recently [that enquiry
mindset] is fresh and I enjoy research' (respondent #4). What's
more responses also indicated that they *felt able to experiment*:
'you can run with stuff and if it works and it gets results [the
headteacher] is happy to go with it … I feel I've got a huge
amount of freedom [to innovate]' (respondent #4).

In terms of the negative codes, it was clear that participants
in this quadrant could *not* point to examples of leadership
support directed at encouraging EIP more widely (*recognises
school/federation level of support for EIP*). They could, however, suggest what support was required if EIP was to materialise at a school or federation level: '[there needs to be] a lot of
communication and … clarity on what staff are going to do
and what they need to go away and do … really clear
objectives … and allocated time provided' (respondent #8).

The code indicating a localised research-use focus was
that of *purpose*, which represented the tension felt by respondents when attempting to meet the micro- and macro-level
demands they regularly faced. Specifically, participants noted
that the focus of the research-use activity needed a recognisable purpose if they were to buy into it. Sometimes this meant
that they felt the focus for EIP should be at the level of the
classroom rather than the level of the federation: 'I think
people have to see the purpose of it … [in the past] I found it

difficult to buy into because I didn't agree on what it was … and I didn't really understand why it was … It has to be something that people believe is worthwhile [whereas in the past] what we actually felt we needed was to make ourselves better prepared [for meeting local needs]' (respondent #4); '[it needs to be] something which is directly important to us and our school' (respondent #12). In part, as is shown below, this may be because of the difficulties faced at the local level (for example some respondents referred to a difficult cohort they had just finished teaching); also the competing priorities that can manifest locally, meaning that any new activity has to be regarded as 100% meaningful, if it is to carry weight.

What's more, the *network orientation* of participants indicated a lack of depth of engagement with others. While those in the Type 1 and Type 2 quadrants employed *networked learning conversations*, those in this quadrant were more likely to engage in more superficial collaboration with networked peers (e.g. Warren Little, 1982). For example, the simple sharing (i.e. cost) of resource, rather than deep engagement with peers that centres on how to use the resource effectively: 'networking [extends to sharing] and using the resources of other schools' (respondent #4); 'being part of a federation, you are sharing expertise, aren't you? Something that [other teacher] does at [other school] and works really well, we can all try' (respondent #13). Likewise, any form of networked collaboration was seen at the level of 'email[ing] each other and keep[ing] in contact' (respondent #13). Occasionally there was active rejection of a networked approach: 'I hope we do it in school, its more of an issue to work across the federation' (respondent #8).

Finally a key issue for those in this quadrant was the number of *competing priorities* that often seemed to 'get in the way' of research-use (the cost vale of *time*). As one respondent noted: 'last year in school we had OFSTED ... I was moderated, we had difficult relations with some parents and children ... I think there has to be space otherwise you can't do it' (respondent #4); 'We haven't time to sit down and talk to each other and communicate with each other ... school is so full-on and so busy' (respondent #12). This led to others noting that their research activity tends to happen 'in our own time' (respondent #6). As highlighted above, the feeling that there were competing priorities, and a lack of time – along with a lack of recognition of any supporting structures or culture for research-use at the school/federation level, reinforced the use of research to tackle only local and immediate classroom level priorities.

With these factors combined, it is perhaps no surprise that when it came to the *signifying* values associated with research-use, respondents within this quadrant tended to articulate a practical purpose. For instance, evidence-use was regarded as a *useful tool* which *provides a route to better student outcomes*. As one respondent noted, the purpose of EIP is: 'having something that you maybe want to address or something that you want to move forward and saying "how can I have a better understanding? How can I make this better or improve this?"' (respondent #4). A research-informed teacher meanwhile was seen as having good pedagogic knowledge (respondent #4): research-use thus seen as providing the basis for *confident professional autonomy*. In keeping with the analysis above, the imagery associated with EIP also had a local focus: 'its using evidence that other people have gathered in your own classroom in your own way' (respondent #13).

*Type 4*: Only one respondent provided responses to suggest that they held Type 4 beliefs. Although these responses were atypical in comparison to those held by other respondents, it is possible to triangulate these codes in relation to the analysis above. Doing so shows that, in terms of *benefit*, unlike with other quadrants, this participant did not *feel able to experiment* (they thus demonstrated a negative *enquiry mindset*). In terms of *cost* value, this respondent also flagged the issue of *competing priorities*. Finally, while respondents located in the other three quadrants universally linked EIP to solving problems, developing an enquiry habit of mind (OECD, 2016), becoming a reflective practitioner and developing twenty-first-century learners, this respondent linked EIP directly to *performativity* and *accountability*.

# REFERENCES

Alton-Lee, A. (2012). The use of evidence to improve education and serve the public good. Paper prepared for the New Zealand Ministry of Education and the annual meeting of the American Educational Research Association, Vancouver Canada, April 2012.

Andreoni, J. (1990). Impure altruism and donations to public goods: A theory of warm-glow giving. *Economic Journal*, *100*, 464–477.

Bacharach, M. (1999). Interactive team reasoning: A contribution to the theory of cooperation. *Research in Economics*, *53*, 117–147.

Bacharach, M. (2006). *Beyond individual choice: Teams and frames in game theory*. Princeton, NJ: Princeton University Press.

Baudrillard, J. (1968). *The system of objects*. London: Verso.

Berger, J. (2016). *Invisible influence: The hidden forces that shape behaviour*. New York, NY: Simon & Schuster.

Bilalić, M., McLeod, P., & Gobet, F. (2008). Why good thoughts block better ones: The mechanism of the pernicious Einstellung (set) effect. *Cognition*, *3*, 652–661.

Brown, C. (2014). *Evidence-informed policy and practice in education: A sociological grounding.* London: Bloomsbury.

Brown, C. (2016). *Scenes, semiotics and the new real: Exploring the value of originality and difference.* London: Palgrave Macmillan.

Brown, C. (2017). *Achieving evidence-informed policy and practice in education: Evidenced.* Bingley: Emerald Publishing.

Brown, C., Schildkamp, K., & Hubers, M. (2017). Combining the best of two worlds: A conceptual proposal for evidence-informed school improvement. *Educational Research*, *59*(2), 154–172.

Brown, C., & Zhang, D. (2016). Is engaging in evidence-informed practice in education rational? Examining the divergence between teachers' attitudes towards evidence use and their actual instances of evidence use in schools. *British Educational Research Journal*, *42*(5), 780–801.

Cain, T. (2015). Teachers' engagement with published research: Addressing the knowledge problem. *Curriculum Journal*, *26*(3), 488–509.

Coldwell, M., Greany, T., Higgins, S., Brown, C., Maxwell, B., Stiell, B., … Burns, H. (2017). *Evidence-informed teaching: An evaluation of progress in England.* Department for Education, London.

CUREE. (2010). Report of professional practitioner use of research review: Practitioner engagement in and/or with research. CUREE, GTCE, LSIS & NTRP, Coventry. Retrieved from http://www.curee-paccts.com/node/2303. Accessed on December 24, 2016.

Daly, A. (2010). Mapping the terrain: Social network theory and educational change. In A. Daly (Ed.), *Social network theory and educational change*. Cambridge, MA: Harvard Education Press.

Dawes, R., van de kragta, M., & Orbell, J. (1988). Not me or thee but we: The importance of group identity in eliciting cooperation in dilemma situations: Experimental manipulation. *Acta Pscychologica, 68*, 83–97.

Eco, U. (1979). *A theory of semiotics*. Bloomington, IN: Indiana University Press.

Eco, U. (2003). *Mouse or rat? Translation as negotiation*. London: Phoenix.

EEF. (2014). EEF launches £1.5 million fund to improve use of research in schools. Retrieved from https://educationen-dowmentfoundation.org.uk/news/eef-launches-15-million-fund-to-improve-use-of-research-in-schools/. Accessed on September 27, 2015.

Elster, J. (2007). *Explaining social behavior: More nuts and bolts for the social sciences*. New York, NY: Cambridge University Press.

Evans, A. (2017). *The myth gap*. London: Eden Project Books.

Galdin-O'Shea, H. (2015). Leading 'disciplined enquiries' in schools. In C. Brown (Ed.), *Leading the use of research & evidence in schools* (pp. 90–105). London: IOE Press.

Godfrey, D. (2014). *Creating a research culture – Lessons from other schools*. Retrieved from http://www.sec-ed.co.uk/best-practice/creating-a-research-culture-lessons-from-other-schools. Accessed on November 22, 2017.

Godfrey, D. (2016). Leadership of schools as research-led organizations in the English educational environment: Cultivating a research engaged school culture, Educational Management Administration & Leadership, early online publication, *44*(2), 301–321.

Goldacre, B. (2013). Building evidence into education. Department for Education, London. Retrieved from https://www.gov.uk/government/news/building-evidence-into-education. Accessed on September 10, 2017.

Greany, T. (2015). How can evidence inform teaching and decision making across 21,000 autonomous schools? Learning from the journey in England. In C. Brown (Ed.), *Leading the use of research & evidence in schools* (pp. 11–29). London: IOE Press.

Green, S. (2002). *Rational choice theory: An overview*. Waco, TX: Baylor University.

Handscomb, G., & MacBeath, J. (2003). The research engaged school. Essex County Council.

Hawkes, T. (1978). *Structuralism and semiotics*. London: Methuen & Co.

Jolls, C., Sunstein, C., & Aler, R. (1998). *A behavioral approach to law and economics*, Faculty Scholarship Series, Paper 1765. Retrieved from http://digitalcommons.law.yale.edu/fss_papers/1765/. Accessed on September 25, 2017.

Kahneman, D. (2003). Maps of bounded rationality: Psychology for behavioral economics. *American Economic Review*, *93*(5), 1449–1475.

Kegan, R., & Lahey, L. (2009). *Immunity to change: How to overcome it and unlock potential in yourself and your organization*. Boston, MA: Harvard Business Press.

Kerr, N. (1992). Efficacy as a causal and moderating variable in social dilemmas. In W. Liebrand, D. Messick, & H. Wilke (Eds.), *Social dilemmas: Theoretical issues and research findings* (pp. 59–80). Oxford: Pergamon.

Latour, B. (1987). *Science in action: How to follow scientists and engineers through society*. Cambridge, MA: Harvard University Press.

Leiserowitz, A., Maibach, E., Roser-Renouf, C., Rosenthal, S., & Cutler, M. (2017). *Climate change in the American mind: May 2017*. Retrieved from http://climatecommunication.yale.edu/wp-content/uploads/2017/07/Climate-Change-American-Mind-May-2017.pdf. Accessed on August 5, 2017.

Lincoln, Y., & Guba, E. (1985). *Naturalistic inquiry*. Newbury Park, CA: Sage Publications.

Lister, R. (2000). To Rio via the 3rd way: Labour's welfare reform agenda. *Renewal: A Journal of Labour Politics (Online)*, 8, 9–20.

Mincu, M. (2014). Inquiry paper 6: Teacher quality and school improvement – What is the role of research? In the British Educational Research Association/The Royal Society for the encouragement of Arts, Manufactures and Commerce (Eds.), *The Role of Research in Teacher Education: Reviewing the Evidence*. Retrieved from https://www.bera.ac.uk/wp-content/uploads/2014/02/BERA-RSA-Interim-Report.pdf. Accessed on November 8, 2017.

Nozick, R. (1974). *Anarchy, state and utopia*. New York, NY: Basic Books.

Nozick, R. (2001). *Invariances: The structure of the objective world*. Cambridge, MA: Harvard University Press.

Nutley, S., Walter, I., & Davies, H. (2002). *From knowing to doing: A framework for understanding the evidence-into-practice agenda*. Retrieved from http://www.ruru.ac.uk/pdf/KnowDo%20paper.pdf. Accessed on November 10, 2017.

Oakley, A. (2000). *Experiments in knowing: Gender and method in the social sciences*. Cambridge: Polity Press.

OECD. (2016). *What makes a school a learning organization*. Retrieved from http://www.oecd.org/education/school/school-learning-organisation.pdf. Accessed on July 25, 2017.

Olson, M. (1965). *The logic of collective action*. Cambridge, MA: Harvard University Press.

Pearce, W., Grundmann, R., Hulme, M., Raman, S., Hadley Kershaw, E., & Tsouvalis, J. (2017). Beyond counting climate consensus. *Environmental Communication*, *11*(6), 723–730.

Petrarca, F. (2008). *Invectives*. Cambridge, MA: Harvard University Press.

Rose, J., & Colman, A. (2007). Collective preferences in strategic decisions. *Psychological Reports*, *101*, 803–815.

Rose, J., Thomas, S., Zhang, L., Edwards, A., Augero, A., & Rooney, P. (2017). *Research learning communities: Evaluation report and executive summary (December 2017)*. Retrieved from https://educationendowmentfoundation.org.uk/public/files/Projects/Evaluation_Reports/Research_Learning_Communities.pdf. Accessed on December 15, 2017.

Saint Augustine. (2002). *On the trinity*. Cambridge: Cambridge University Press.

Sartre, J.-P. (2013). *Existentialism and humanism*. York: Methuen.

Scruton, R. (1982). *Kant*. Oxford: Oxford University Press.

Sebba, J., Tregenza, J., & Kent, P. (2012). *Powerful professional learning: A school leader's guide to joint practice development*. Nottingham: National College for School Leadership.

Sen, A. (1990). Rational behaviour. In J. Eatwell, M. Milgate, & P. Newman (Eds.), *Utility and probability* (pp. 198–216). New York, NY: W. W. Norton.

Stoll, L. (2015). *Three greats for a self-improving school system: Pedagogy, professional development and leadership: Executive summary*. Retrieved from https://www.gov.uk/government/uploads/system/uploads/attachment_data/file/406279/Three_greats_for_a_self_improving_system_pedagogy_professional_development_and_leadership_executive_summary.pdf. Accessed on February 27, 2015.

Stoll, L., Bolam, R., McMahon, A., Wallace, M., & Thomas, S. (2006). Professional learning communities: A review of the literature. *Journal of Educational Change*, 7(4), 221–258.

van der Linden, S., Leiserowitz, A., Feinberg, G., & Maibach, E. (2015). The scientific consensus on climate change as a gateway belief: Experimental evidence. *PLoS ONE*, *10*, 2. Retrieved from http://journals.plos.org/plosone/article?id=10.1371/journal.pone.0118489. Accessed on November 24, 2017.

Vico, G. (2002). *The first new science*. L. Pompa (Ed.). Cambridge, Cambridge University Press.

Whitty, G., & Wisby, E. (2017). Is evidence-informed practice any more feasible than evidence-informed policy?

Presented at the British Educational Research Association
annual conference, Sussex, 5–7 September, 2017.

Williams, B. (1981). Internal and external reasons. In B.
Williams (Ed.), *Moral luck: Philosophical papers 1973–1980*
(pp. 101–113). Cambridge: Cambridge University Press.

# INDEX